A COASTAL POND

Studied by Oceanographic Methods

A COASTAL POND

Studied by Oceanographic Methods

K. O. EMERY

Woods Hole Oceanographic Institution, Woods Hole, Massachusetts

AMERICAN ELSEVIER PUBLISHING COMPANY, INC.
NEW YORK 1969

American Elsevier Publishing Company, Inc.
52 Vanderbilt Avenue
New York, N.Y. 10017

Elsevier Publishing Company
Barking, Essex, England

Elsevier Publishing Company
335 Jan Van Galenstraat, P.O. Box 211
Amsterdam, The Netherlands

Standard Book Number 444–00050–X

Library of Congress Card Number 73–75526

Printed in The United States of America

To My Colleagues

Who Gave Freely of Their Time

Preface

The large funding and the complex expeditions of recent years tend to cause the problems of oceanography to be overshadowed by the means for solving them. Many of the problems can be studied cheaply and easily in the model oceans of coastal ponds. Some geological, chemical, biological, and physical characteristics are nearly the same as in the ocean, or they may be closely related to the adjacent part of the ocean. In other ways, the ponds are important in their own right as sites for measuring increased coastal pollution, as contributors of nutrients to the ocean, and as essential parts in the life histories of many animals; although much has been written about their ecological importance, knowledge of coastal ponds and marshes is still inadequate.

The study of Oyster Pond was a low-cost backyard operation, but it cut through much of the whole field of oceanography. The scientific opportunities, the low costs, and the widespread occurrence of such ponds suggest that they may serve as useful environments for investigation during the present period of rapid growth of oceanographic education in the United States and in many other countries. Many problems to be found in the ponds appeal to the naturalist (or generalist), some belong to the specialist, but most can cause both generalist and specialist to appreciate each other's approach and methods. It is hoped that the examples of low-cost research presented in this study will motivate budding oceanographers to go beyond the classroom and onto the water.

K. O. EMERY

Woods Hole, Massachusetts
February, 1969

Contents

List of Tables

List of Figures

1 Introduction

More than one hundred lakes dot the landscape of Cape Cod. They have highly irregular shapes and range from mere puddles to areas of several square kilometers. The lakes lie in basins that once were occupied by large irregular chunks of ice, remnants of a thick and continuous cover of glaciers on the cape. When the ice melted it not only produced lake basins on the cape, but the meltwater from glaciers there and elsewhere in the world caused the sea level to rise. As the shore advanced, the lake basins around the perimeter of the cape were drowned by sea water and filled with sediments carried by ocean waves and currents. Oyster Pond (Figs. 1 and 2) at the present shore between Woods Hole and Falmouth, Massachusetts, was reached by the

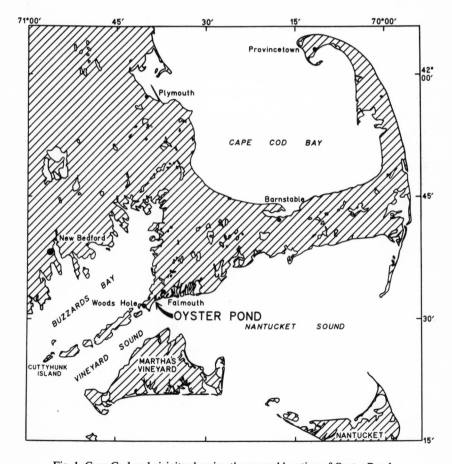

Fig. 1. Cape Cod and vicinity showing the general location of Oyster Pond.

1

ocean only a few thousand years ago. Its sediments still preserve the record of its fresh-water history, and its waters are intermediate between those of fresh-water lakes and the adjacent Nantucket and Vineyard Sounds, where the advancing sea already has won its contest over the land. The continued rise of sea level eventually will cause Oyster Pond to be submerged and then other lakes that still are untouched by the ocean will be reached.

Beginning in the summer of 1962 the author has made his home at the head of Oyster Pond. Many observations could easily be made over a period of several years. Even more important, many scientists at the nearby Woods Hole Oceanographic Institution and the Marine Biological Laboratory became interested in extending to the pond special techniques that they had developed for general investigations of the geology, biology, chemistry, and water movements of the ocean. Contributions by members of this large group of specialists are noted in appropriate sections of the text.

2 Geology

Inspection of Fig. 2 shows that Oyster Pond is cut off from the ocean by a baymouth bar. We might presume from the former glaciation and the presence of the bar that the area was once a fresh-water pond, then an open bay, an estuary, and now again a pond—but one closely associated with the ocean. A careful investigation of its topography and sediments should reveal evidence of each major stage of its history; a discussion of this evidence is one of the objectives of this little book.

Fig. 2. An aerial photograph of Oyster Pond, which shows the relationship of the pond to Vineyard Sound (foreground) and Buzzards Bay (background). The connection of the pond with Vineyard Sound is presently through the series of smaller ponds and a conduit between the short jetties at the left margin of the photograph. (Made in 1964 by W. D. Athearn.)

The shores of the pond are of three kinds. Most, 70%, are steeply sloping to a height of 5 to 10 meters above the pond and are marked by a line of boulders along the water's edge. At the southeastern side and comprising about 12% of the perimeter, the shore is less steep, only a few meters high, and it is bordered by gravel but by few boulders. Along the south and south-western sides and locally elsewhere at the mouths of small tributary valleys, the shore consists of low grassy marshes; these constitute about 18% of the total perimeter. The first kind of shore is covered with oak forest, the second has chiefly bushes and other plants introduced for home landscaping, and the third has reeds and fresh-water grasses.

3

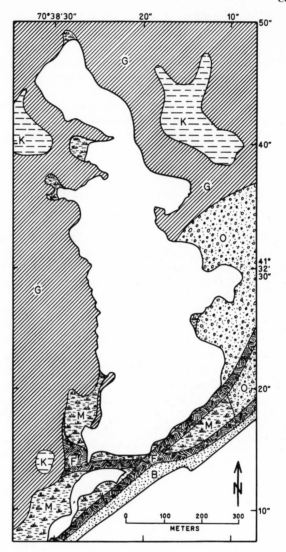

Fig. 3. Physiographic units of the land adjacent to Oyster Pond. Symbols are as follows:
G—glacial till, K—kettles, O—outwash plain, M—marsh, B—beach, and F—artificial fill.

Closer examination shows that the first kind of shore is backed by glacial till
(Fig. 3) consisting of boulders, ranging in length to more than 4 meters, which
are embedded in gravel and coarse sand. Most are granite and gneiss. The till
belongs to the Buzzards Bay recessional moraine which extends southwesterly
through Woods Hole and along the Elizabeth Islands (Shaler, 1897; Woodworth and Wigglesworth, 1934, pl. 1, 6; Mather, Goldthwait, and Theis-

meyer, 1942). It is considered to be Middle Wisconsin in age by Kaye (1964). Farther south are several earlier glacial deposits including moraines on Martha's Vineyard, Nantucket, and the sea floor. Fronting each of the hummocky moraines is a wide and relatively flat outwash plain composed of sands and gravels deposited by glacial meltwater streams. One of these plains backs the second kind of pond shore.

Masses of ice from an early advanced position of the Buzzards Bay glacier remained unmelted for a time to become partly buried under outwash from the Buzzards Bay moraine. When these masses finally melted, kettle pond depressions remained in the outwash plain. This gave rise to the term Mashpee Pitted Plain. The north end of Oyster Pond is a kettle left by the melting of a residual mass of glacial ice within the Buzzards Bay moraine. Its southward extension consists of two other kettles that mark the former positions of ice masses within the outwash plain. The north-south alignment of the kettles, giving rise to the elongate shape of the pond, probably resulted from some control of ice thickness and movement exerted by north–south preglacial stream valleys [suggested by Shaler (1897)]. Some of the 15 or more elongate ponds in the 15 km of coast east of Oyster Pond also are associated with kettles, but most of them occupy drowned valleys cut into the outwash plain by streams from melting ice or melting permafrost.

The total thickness of Pleistocene deposits in the area of Oyster Pond is unknown, but it probably is about 80 meters. A foundation test boring made during August 1965 for a pier at Woods Hole Oceanographic Institution about 4 km southwest of Oyster Pond encountered granodiorite at 83 meters below mean low water. It was overlain by 81 meters of clean sand, probably glacial outwash, and by 2 meters of sea water. The rock is considered to be the Dedham Granodiorite that crops out extensively along the western shore of Buzzards Bay (Emerson, 1917, pl. 1). Its depth is supported by seismic refraction velocities of 5440 meters per second obtained by Ewing, Crary, and Rutherford (1937, table 3) below depths of 90 meters beneath sea level at Woods Hole, and by similar velocities measured by Oldale and Tuttle (1964) about 47 meters below sea level 10 km northeast of Woods Hole. Elsewhere in the region the granodiorite and the Pleistocene deposits may be separated by a few meters of Miocene greensand (as on the nearby islands), by Eocene silt (as encountered in wells at eastern Cape Cod by Zeigler, Hoffmeister, Geise, and Tasha, 1960), or by Cretaceous clay, sandstone, and lignite coal (as on the islands).

3 Human Occupation of the Region

Indians had lived on Cape Cod for probably thousands of years prior to the arrival of Europeans. Mute witness is provided by at least three large burying grounds in and near Falmouth. Contacts between Indians and Europeans may have occurred early in the 16th century (Emerson, 1935; Howe, 1943), but the first semi-detailed accounts of the coast near Falmouth and Woods Hole were those of 1602 by the colonist Bartholomew Gosnold and his associates Gabriel Archer and John Brereton (Gookin and Barbour, 1963). Arriving aboard the *CONCORD* from Falmouth, England, they spent about a month (14th May to 17 June) in the region, which included landings on Martha's Vineyard, the Elizabeth Islands, and the mainland.

Eighteen years after Gosnold's landing the Pilgrims settled at Plymouth, only 45 km north of Oyster Pond. The well-known religious intolerance of most of those who settled the New World for religious "freedom" soon caused Quakers, Catholics, and other minority groups to have difficulties. Isaac Robinson, a Quaker or a friend of the Quakers, thus was forced to leave Barnstable (an outlying settlement of Plymouth), and with Jonathon Hatch and a few others he settled about 1 km east of Oyster Pond in 1660 (Clarke and Holton, 1887; Jenkins, 1889; Geoffrey, 1930). Within a year land was purchased from the local Indians, and it was divided and farmed. One of the first pieces of land to be portioned was that immediately east of Oyster Pond (Freeman, 1862, p. 427; Faught, 1945, p. 24). By 1668 the settlement was incorporated under the name Suckanesset, "where the black wampum is found" (black wampum was made from the black or dark purple spot in the shells of quahaug clams—Forbes, 1934). By 1693 the name had been changed to Falmouth (Walton, 1925), Gosnold's port of departure from England.

According to Freeman (1862, p. 448) and Jenkins (1889, p. 57), the townspeople originally obtained an abundance of oysters from Oyster Pond, thus accounting for its name. Oysters evidently were common at many places in Cape Cod as shown by many shell heaps left by the Indians and by the use of oysters by settlers beginning with the Pilgrims (see also Thoreau's "Wellfleet Oysterman"). Their decrease and near-extinction in the region may have been due to overexploitation or diseases (Kittredge, 1930, pp. 203–205). One of the first areas for extinction appears to have been Oyster Pond, because special committees were appointed at town meetings in 1767 and 1773 to investigate the cause of oyster diminution there. Although the reports of the committees are unrecorded, it is possible that the major factor was closure of an inlet from the ocean. In order for the pond water to have been of high enough salinity to support oysters [22 to 32 parts per thousand ($‰$)], the pond originally must have been open to the entrance of sea water. Growth of a baymouth bar during the late 18th century may have closed off the pond and caused it to become too fresh for oysters. A small-scale map published about 1663 by William Hack (Emerson, 1935, p. 63) shows the pond to be open. More detailed maps of 1795 and 1841 definitely show a drainage channel

6

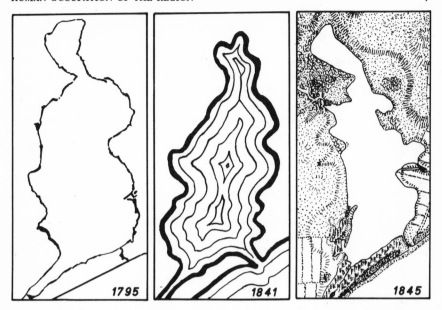

Fig. 4. Redrawn portions of three old large-scale maps. *Left*—Part of map of "Town of Falmouth" dated 20 May 1795 and signed by Selectmen Shiverick, Hatch, and Swift. (From photostat in Library of Congress.) *Middle*—Part of "Plan of the Town of Falmouth in the County of Barnstable" surveyed in 1841 by Jesse Boyden. (From photostat of original in Massachusetts Archives of Maps and Plans, Boston.) *Right*—Part of U.S. Coast and Geodetic Survey's topographic sheet 191 of 1845.

Fig. 5. Photograph of 1895 of north end of Oyster Pond. (From Washburn, 1897, p. 27.)

through the east end of the bar, and a much better map of 1845 by the Coast and Geodetic Survey confirms this drainage and contains topographic details indicative of a former broad opening to the adjacent Vineyard Sound (Fig. 4). There is reported to have been a drainage pipe through the bar in about the same area as late as about 1930. Closure, which transformed a bay into the pond, probably resulted from natural processes. Longshore drift of beach sand toward the east occurs at present, as illustrated by sand piling up against groins that cross the beach. Closure was made more permanent by the building of a railroad embankment in 1872 (Deyo, 1890, p. 127; Faught, 1945) and of a road along the bar about the same date. During the hurricanes of 1938 and 1944 waves cut through the bar and railroad embankment at or near the opening indicated by the early maps. Their effect is revealed by dislodged rails and ties still protruding from the pond side of the rebuilt railroad embankment, and possibly by washover fans in the same area.

Near Oyster Pond the original forest-covered land was cleared for agriculture and grazing probably soon after 1660, with much of the timber being used as fuel for glass making, and later for the railroad. Photographs of Oyster Pond made about 1895 (Board of Trade and Industry, 1896; Washburn, 1897) show the land east of the pond to be almost bare of trees (Fig. 5). By 1925 (Walton, 1925, p. 18) trees had reclaimed most of this area, except just at the north end of the pond. The presence or absence of the trees must have been reflected by greater or lesser contributions of organic matter to the pond sediments.

Construction of houses since about 1915 (Fig. 2) resulted in minor changes of the shoreline through the building of about 600 meters of loose stone seawalls and by the dumping of debris to increase lot sizes along about 200 meters of shore.

4 Topography

Oyster Pond is about 1050 meters long and is oriented north-northwest almost at right angles to the shore of Vineyard Sound. The maximum width of the pond is 400 meters, but because the shores are very irregular the average width is about half that figure. Its total surface area is 0.250 km² (62 acres) (Figs. 6 and 7).

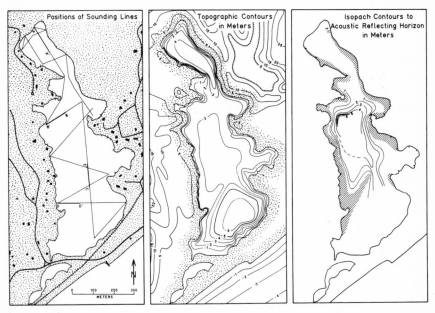

Fig. 6. Topography of Oyster Pond and vicinity. *Left*—Culture and positions of sounding traverses made with H. E. Edgerton's Acoustic Bottom Penetrator. Lettered parts of the traverses are reproduced in Fig. 8. (Pond outline, roads, and most of the houses are from aerial photograph DPL–2K–145 made on 22 October 1951 by the Department of Agriculture.) *Middle*—Bottom topography contoured on basis of sounding traverses supplemented by spot soundings. Base level for both the pond and adjacent sea floor is the common level of the pond, about 0.30 meter above the mean sea level used for land contours and about 0.50 meter above the mean low water level used for most hydrographic surveys. *Right*—Topography of a velocity discontinuity detected as a subbottom reflection by the Acoustic Bottom Penetrator. Cross-hatching indicates areas where the bottom consists largely of boulders.

The south end of the pond was formerly a sand and gravel bar which separated it from the sound, but a railroad embankment and a highway fill built along the north side of the bar and atop an adjoining marsh now limits the pond. An extension of the marsh has developed on washover fans produced by high waves of hurricanes. Between the railroad and the highway are several small, shallow (0.5-meter deep) marsh lagoons which extend 350

9

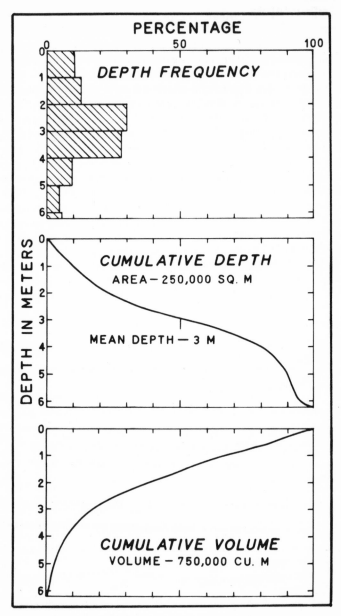

Fig. 7. Hypsometric curves of area and volume of Oyster Pond based upon the bottom contours of Fig. 6. Note that the permanent sill of the basin is about 25 cm lower than the indicated zero level of the figure; the effective sill is a fill of sand and gravel in a conduit under the railroad and through the baymouth bar that separates Oyster Pond from Vineyard Sound.

meters southwest of the pond. The pond drains into the first marsh lagoon through a conduit under the highway at the southwestern corner of the pond, and the marsh lagoon in turn connects with the open sound through another conduit under the railroad and a trench through the bar 200 meters southwest of the pond (near the south-western corner of Fig. 6).

On 29 August 1963, a general topographic survey of Oyster Pond was made in company with Harold E. Edgerton (Massachusetts Institute of Technology) using his Acoustic Bottom Penetrator. This device is a portable continuous seismic profiler operated at 12 kc with a signal pulse length of 0.1 msec and recording on a scale of 2 meters per centimeter of paper width. A total track length of 3600 meters (Fig. 6) was sounded from a boat rowed at an average speed of about 1 km per hour between known shore points. About 30 spot soundings were made close to the acoustic ones to serve as checks on the latter. Twenty additional spot soundings, some taken during bottom sampling operations, completed the coverage of the pond. The datum base level is that of the common level of the pond, 50 cm above mean low water of the adjacent sound and about 25 cm above the bottom of the conduit beneath the railroad.

The first or bottom echo provided information on the water depths, as shown by contours of Fig. 6. The slopes near shore are the steepest, commonly 2°, although less steep than the adjacent shores whose contours were

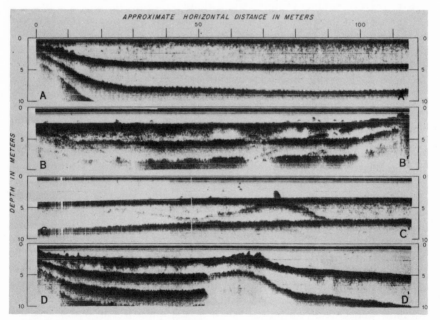

Fig. 8. Examples of records obtained by the Acoustic Bottom Penetrator. Note the generally flat bottom of panel A, the sub-bottom reflections of panels B and C, and the boulder-covered ridge in panel D. Proper interpretation requires recognition of the several multiple reflections from the bottom of the pond. Positions of the profiles are given in Fig. 6.

interpolated from those of the U.S. Geological Survey's Woods Hole topographic quadrangle. No evidence of a subaqueous wave-cut or wave-built terrace was noted. At the middle of the pond the bottom is nearly horizontal; thus the profile is essentially broadly concave. The contours show that the pond contains three separate basins. The northern one is small, narrow, and has a maximum depth of 4.5 meters along much of its length. The sill which separates it from the middle basin is about 130 meters south of the narrowest part of the pond and is about 2.5 meters deep. Occupying the middle and widest part of the pond is the middle basin. This is not a closed depression but a broad and fairly flat area having maximum depths of only 3.2 meters except near its southern end where the bottom deepens toward the southern basin. The southern basin is intermediate in size, slightly elongate, and is parallel to the shore of the sound. Maximum depths of 6.2 meters occur near its center, the deepest area of the entire pond. Thus, Oyster Pond consists of three basins, the deepest at the south, the intermediate at the north, and a broad shallower area between them. The total volume of water in the pond is about 750,000 cubic meters.

Most of the profiles exhibit irregularities of 0.5 to 1.0 meter near shore (Fig. 8, B and D). In many places these irregularities were found, by probing, to be boulders exposed above the general level of the bottom. As shown by Fig. 6, areas of boulder bottom extend along both sides of the pond, but they do not occur at the ends of it. Irregularities in shallow water at the north end of the pond (Fig. 8, A) were noted on the acoustic profiler, but they consist only of submerged algae and logs. Other irregularities in deep water were judged to be submerged logs, but some of them may be boulders.

The acoustic profiles also show subbottom reflections near the north end of the middle basin beneath as much as 6 meters of sediment (assuming the velocity of sound to be the same in the sediment as in the overlying water), or at a total depth of 8.5 meters below the surface of the pond. This reflecting horizon was found throughout the middle basin except where it was obscured by the second or third multiple reflection of the bottom. At the south end of the middle basin the subbottom reflection shoals markedly to form a northeast–southwest-trending ridge which extends more than half way across the pond. As shown by Fig. 8 (C), where the subbottom reflections rise to intersect the bottom of the pond, boulders project sharply about one meter higher to a water depth of only 2.7 meters. Poor subbottom reflections in both the north and south basins probably were caused by the presence of gas bubbles in the sediments.

The bottom contours of Oyster Pond accord with the glacial origin of the pond inferred from the topography and geology of the surroundings. The pond's northern basin is a glacial kettle within the Buzzards Bay terminal moraine and contains a partial fill of lake sediment. The middle basin is probably a similar kettle but one filled to overflowing with sediment probably from both the glacial outwash and the subsequent lake. Between the middle and southern basins is an elongate ridge extending between the known front of the Buzzards Bay moraine on either side of the pond. Its position, shape, and cover of boulders indicate that the ridge must be a submerged part of the moraine. The elliptical shape of the contours of the basin south of the moraine strongly suggests that this basin, like the other two, is a kettle; but one whose shape was modified by construction of the sand and gravel bar. The presence of this third basin beyond the terminal moraine accords with the suggestion that it was left by tardy melting of a remnant of ice after partial burial under outwash from the Buzzards Bay moraine.

5 Sediments

GRAIN-SIZE DISTRIBUTION

Thirty-two sediment samples were collected from Oyster Pond and the adjacent marsh lagoons, sea floor, and soils (Fig. 9) on 21 September 1963. The underwater samples were taken with a light-weight van Veen sampler having a capacity of about 1 liter. Positions estimated from distances and bearings of the many identifiable shore points are believed to be accurate to within 10 or 20 meters depending upon the locality. After a brief field description was recorded, a half-liter portion of the sample was placed in an ice-cream carton for laboratory analyses. Colors of the wet samples were estimated the following day using the rock color chart of Goddard and others (1948). Grain-size determinations were made by John Schlee using a combination of pipette analysis for the silt and clay fraction and settling tube (Schlee, 1966) analysis for the sand fraction.

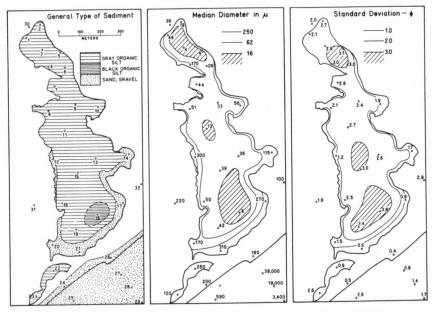

Fig. 9. Bottom materials of Oyster Pond and vicinity. *Left*—Positions and numbers of samples, with field descriptions of sediments. *Middle*—Median diameters in microns. *Right*—Phi standard deviation (sorting) of grain distributions of sediments.

Most of the pond is floored with olive gray (5Y3/3) silt which contains much organic matter, in the form of a gray organic silt (Fig. 9). Black organic silt was noted only at station 18 in the deepest part of the pond. Generally, the greater the depth, the smaller the median diameter of the silt; in fact, the

14

sediment of the northern basin almost reaches the grain-size limit of clay (finer than 4 μ). A decrease in median diameter is accompanied by poorer sorting, leading to ϕ standard deviations greater than 3.0 for the finest sediment. At station 18, beneath about 5 cm of black organic silt is a 4-cm layer of medium gray sand (median diameter of 280 μ) and cinders which measure up to 3 cm diameter. Presumably the sand and cinders were swept into the pond by sea waves of the 1938 hurricane.

Sands near the shores of the pond vary from fine to very coarse grained and range from greenish gray (5GY5/1) to yellowish brown (10YR3/2). They are residual concentrates of coarser components of glacial till and outwash sorted by wave action. Little sand reaches the pond by way of streams, because the few intermittent streams which empty into the pond enter through marshes that effectively trap the sands. Most marine sands on the baymouth bar south of the pond are even coarser and better sorted; they range from yellowish gray (5Y8/1) on the sea beach to dark yellowish brown (10YR4/2) on the sea floor, where they are accompanied by gravels having the same color. These marine sands result from the same residual concentration as the nearshore sands within the pond, but are sorted by the far larger and more effective waves of Vineyard and Nantucket Sounds.

MINERAL COMPOSITION

Coarse fractions (> 62 μ diameter) of the samples were examined with the aid of the binocular microscope. The detrital minerals are similar in all samples, with quartz grains dominant. Most quartz grains in the pond muds are finer than about 150 μ and they are angular and clear. Also present are a few much coarser quartz grains (usually > 2 mm) that have rounded and frosted surfaces. The sands near the shore of the pond and along the beaches of Vineyard Sound contain larger concentrations of the rounded and frosted grains, and the very coarse sands of the sound have the greatest abundance of them. The coarse fractions also contain cloudy feldspars, occasional flakes of muscovite, and a variety of colored and black heavy minerals, but the concentration of all nonquartz detrital minerals was estimated to be less than about 5% by volume of the total coarse fraction. The general composition of the detrital part of the coarse fraction is about what should be expected of outwash from glaciers that had crossed a region of intrusive igneous and metamorphic rocks such as those of New England. The large rounded and frosted quartz grains probably were shaped by sand blast produced by periglacial winds.

Most interesting in the coarse fraction are the black grains of nondetrital origin. All the samples from the pond floor contain numerous flakes and irregular pieces of charcoal, and are distinguished by a fibrous texture and/or a soft and easily crushed nature. These grains are the remains of the stems, leaves, and seeds of land plants that became oxidized either by fire on shore or by slower oxidation within the pond sediments. Two samples (Nos. 2 and 4 of Fig. 9) contain large flakes of hard black material that is yellow to red on their flat surfaces; this material is hematite partly altered to limonite, and it was produced either from oxidation of iron scrap that had been thrown into the pond, or from authigenic precipitation of bog iron. A third kind of black grain is hard, brittle, glassy, contains numerous pores, and ranges to more than 1 cm in diameter. These grains are cinders and they are most abundant in samples 15 through 23 from localities that are the closest to the railroad track. Some of them may have come from the smoke of the locomotives which pulled trains along the tracks between 1872 and 1965. However, the concentration of cinders within the sand layer at station 18 (Fig. 9) at the deepest point of the pond probably indicates that most of the cinders were washed from the cinder track ballast by high sea waves during hurricanes. Occasional semicubic grains of anthracite coal are associated with the cinders in some samples, attesting the railroad source of the cinders.

TABLE 1
Heavy Minerals in Sand Fractions

	No. 30 Soil	No. 1 North Basin	No. 18 South Basin	No. 24 Beach
% Heavy Minerals	0.9	0.6	1.5	0.6
Unstable Minerals				
Epidote	47	33	15	21
Hornblende	26	43	16	16
Sillimanite	4	4	4	7
Zoisite	2	2	2	2
Augite	0	2	0	3
Hypersthene	0	1	0	0
	— 79	— 85	— 37	— 49
Stable Minerals				
Garnet	7	7	20	12
Staurolite	4	5	24	17
Tourmaline	2	2	13	13
Titanite	1	1	3	4
Andalusite	1	0	2	4
Zircon	4	0	1	1
Rutile	2	0	0	0
	— 21	— 15	— 63	— 51
Total Non-opaque	100	100	100	100
Opaque	125	47	200	93
Mica	Abdt.	—	—	Some
Altered	3	24	72	31
Unknown	1	2	4	3

Heavy minerals of the sand fraction in four samples were separated from the light minerals by settling in bromoform (specific gravity of 2.89). After being weighed and mounted on glass slides, the minerals were identified by D. A. Ross, who used standard optical techniques. The results (Table 1) show that heavy minerals range from 0.6 to 1.5 % of total sand in the samples, a typical range for glacial, fluvial, and marine sediments of the Cape Cod region. The highest percentage, at the floor of the southern basin, is probably the result of an affinity of heavy minerals for fine-grained well-sorted sand, such as is present there.

Some differences in percentage abundance of different minerals appear to be a function of the different rigors of mechanical abrasion at the different sample localities. Thus, unstable minerals are relatively more abundant in a soil on glacial outwash at the head of the pond and in the sediments of the northern basin than they are on the ocean beach and on the floor of the southern basin (where they probably were carried from the beach by hurricane waves). Conversely, the stable minerals are more abundant on the beach and the floor of the southern basin. The general heavy-mineral composition of the samples is the same as that which Ross (1967) found to be widespread on the sea floor just east of Cape Cod.

TABLE 2
Percentage Compositions of Fine Fractions of Bottom Sediments

Material	Fractions	
	$2-62\,\mu$	$<2\,\mu$
Quartz	60	tr
Feldspar	25	tr
Pyrite	5	2
Illite	5	20
Kaolinite	5	20
Chlorite	tr	tr
Vermiculite	tr	tr
Amorphous silica	0	45

The mineral composition of the fine fraction of samples from stations 3 and 18 was determined by J. C. Hathaway using X-ray diffraction techniques. The results for the two samples were so similar that they are presented together in Table 2. Quartz and feldspar dominate the $2-62\,\mu$ fraction but occur only as traces in the finest fraction. In contrast, the clay minerals illite and kaolinite are about equally abundant at about 20% of the $<2\,\mu$ fraction and at only 5% of the $2-62\,\mu$ fraction. Chlorite and dioctahedral vermiculite occur as traces. A small percentage of pyrite is present. Perhaps most striking is amorphous silica, with an abundance which appears to be 40 or 50% (indicated as 45% in Table 2) of the $<2\,\mu$ size fraction and an absence in the $2-62\,\mu$ fraction. The finer fraction averages 33% of the total weight of the sediment; thus the amorphous silica must constitute about 15% of the whole sediment. Electron micrographs reveal the presence of so many broken frustules of diatoms (Fig. 10) that they must be the major form of the silica.

Another method for learning something of the composition of the sediment is through measurement of gamma radiation. Such measurements made by Claire L. Schelske for two samples (wet state) show marked differences for the gamma ray energy of potassium-40. The considerably greater peak for the sandy sample 26 than for the silty sample 3 is probably due to its greater concentration of the potassium-bearing minerals orthoclase and biotite.

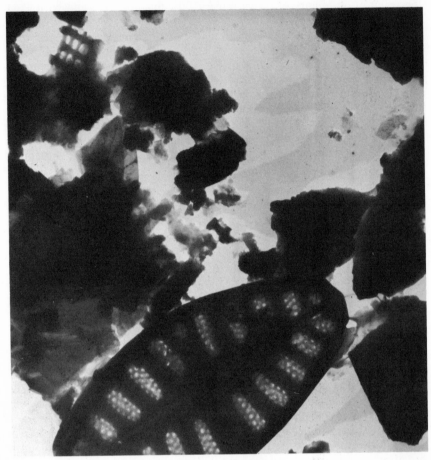

Fig. 10. Electron micrograph showing the presence of broken diatom frustules associated with clay minerals at station 3. (Made by J. C. Hathaway.)

ORGANIC MATTER

Many of the bottom samples from the pond contain oak leaves, twigs, and even large sticks. A few snags that rise to the water surface from depths of about 2 meters reveal the presence of tree trunks that had floated until they became water logged. Along the north shore are many dead but still rooted trunks of bushes whose eroded tops are 5 to 15 cm below the general level of the pond; they mark the presence of former shoreline vegetation killed probably by submergence due to the raising of the pond level when conduits were constructed under the railroad and highway embankments. It is evident that the organic matter in the sediment is due to incomplete oxidation of debris from plants which grow in the pond and from tree leaves which are blown into the pond during autumn.

The percentages of general organic constituents (carbonate, nitrogen, and organic carbon) in sediment samples were determined by Jobst Hülsemann. Carbonate was measured gasometrically and computed as calcium carbonate. Percentages of calcium carbonate range from 0.4 to 3.5 and average only 1.0% within the pond sediments. An average of 0.5% occurs in soils near the pond, indicating that probably some of the calcium carbonate is detrital. The higher values within the pond and the fact that they occur in the finest sediments of highest organic content (Fig. 11) show that most of the calcium carbonate must be biogenic within the pond.

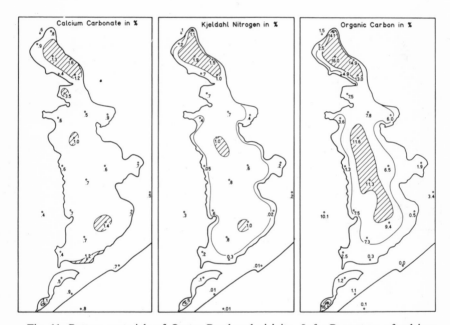

Fig. 11. Bottom materials of Oyster Pond and vicinity. *Left*—Percentage of calcium carbonate, from gasometric analyses for carbonate. *Middle*—Percentage of Kjeldahl nitrogen. *Right*—Percentage of organic carbon (difference between the value of total carbon measured gasometrically after heating of sample in an induction furnace and the value of carbon from carbonate determination).

Nitrogen measured by Kjeldahl distillation is very high in the pond sediments, ranging from 0.02 to 1.85% and averaging 0.65%. Highest values occur in the finest sediment (Fig. 11) and in the small northern basin. Concentrations in the soil are much lower, averaging 0.21%. Similar relationships exist for organic carbon (Fig. 11), which ranges from 0.2 to 16.0% and averages 7.0% in the pond sediments, higher than the 5.0% average for the soils.

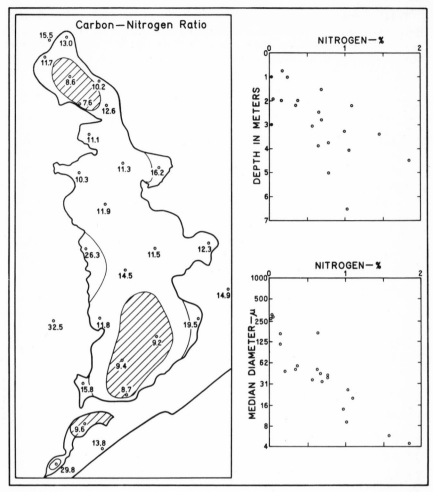

Fig. 12. Relationship of percentage nitrogen in sediments of Oyster Pond to organic carbon, depth, and median diameter of sediments.

Admixture of high-carbon cellulosic debris from land vegetation may account for the high carbon/nitrogen ratio of 29.8 in the sediments of one of the small outlet ponds and of ratios exceeding 15.0 in several nearshore samples from Oyster Pond (Fig. 12). In contrast, the deeper areas having a sediment of finer grain size and higher organic content are characterized by carbon/nitrogen ratios smaller than 10.0. The average ratio for all samples of pond sediment is 12.4. This figure is higher than the average of 10.0 for surface sediments of the southern California basins (Emery, 1960, p. 276), where the organic matter is almost entirely of marine origin.

Total organic matter at station 18 was found by weight loss of two samples during ashing at 600° for 6 hours, after they had been dried at 110°C for 24 hours. The results (Walsh, 1965a) were 19.05 and 19.26%, or an average of 19.15%. The organic carbon found at the same station (Fig. 11) was 9.4%. Thus, the ratio of total organic matter to organic carbon is 2.04.

STABLE CARBON ISOTOPES

The ratio of the stable carbon isotopes, C^{12} and C^{13}, was determined for eleven samples from Oyster Pond by W. M. Sackett and was expressed in the usual terms of δC^{13} (Fig. 13). Results for the organic carbon in eight samples ranged from -22.8 to -25.1 ‰. This was near the middle of the range found for organic carbon in deep-sea sediments, in basin sediments off southern California, and in nearshore sediments of the Gulf of Mexico. No relationship to the carbon/nitrogen ratio of the pond sediments was present. The range of δC^{13} for the pond sediment also corresponds to those for land plants, of single-celled marine plants, and of petroleum. The only marine plants reported to have δC^{13} well outside of the range are multi-celled ones, most of which are attached to the bottom.

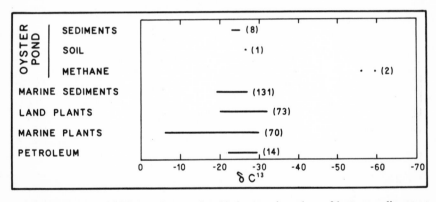

Fig. 13. Ranges of δC^{13} in soil at station 30, in organic carbon of bottom sediment at stations 1, 3, 7, 11, 12, 16, 17, and 18, and in methane from bottom sediment at stations 1 and 3 (Fig. 9). These ranges are compared with those of other environments and materials, as listed by Landegren (1954), Silverman and Epstein (1958), Emery (1960, pp. 288–291), Sackett (1964), and Sackett, Eckelmann, Bender, and Bé (1965). Numbers in parentheses indicate the number of analyses on which each range is based.

The single measurement for soil indicates a slight enrichment of C^{12}, but the two for methane from the bottom sediment exhibit marked enrichment of C^{12}. The latter is probably the result of initial stages of bacterial decomposition of organic matter, whereby a lighter isotope tends to react more quickly than a heavier one [as previously measured for sulfur compounds by Kaplan, Emery, and Rittenberg (1963)].

TABLE 3
Amino Acids in Sediments of Oyster Pond as Compared with those in Two Marine Basins

	μg/gm dry weight			
	Station 3	Station 18	Santa Barbara Basin	San Diego Trough
Basic				
Arginine	203	210	20	177
Histidine	112	115	tr	66
Lysine	379	407	64	435
Hydroxylysine	0	0	n.d.	n.d.
Ornithine	0	0	n.d.	75
Neutral				
α-Alanine	484	490	15	349
β-Alanine	35	90	n.d.	38
Glycine	595	570	38	423
Leucine	378	360	56	335
Alloisoleucine	10	8	n.d.	n.d.
Isoleucine	203	206	204	n.d.
Proline	381	419	tr	318
Hydroxyproline	tr	tr	tr	n.d.
Serine	532	519	7	223
Threonine	424	396	24	206
Valine	328	366	20	308
Acidic				
Aspartic acid	877	876	86	2
Glutamic acid	666	691	22	26
Aromatic				
Phenylalanine	238	262	tr	121
Dihydroxyphenylalanine	0	0	n.d.	n.d.
Tyrosine	180	164	6	79
Sulfur				
Cystine (half)	31	32	16	n.d.
Methionine	46	63	tr	n.d.
Amino Sugars and others				
Glucosamine	448	384	n.d.	n.d.
Galactosamine	106	132	n.d.	n.d.
Diaminopimelic acid	20	20	n.d.	n.d.
α-, β-, γ-Aminobutyric acid	tr	tr	n.d.	n.d.
Total Amino Acids	6676	6780	578	3181
Kjeldahl Nitrogen	19,000	10,000	3310	3200
Amino Acid Nitrogen	874	891	76	51
Ammonia Nitrogen	151	202	53	n.d.

AMINO ACIDS

Two samples of the bottom sediments from Oyster Pond were analyzed for total amino acids, amino sugars, and related compounds by E. T. Degens. The results (Table 3) reveal a wide range of amino acids whose total concentration is almost identical at the sites of stations 3 and 18 (Fig. 9), but exceptionally high for marine sediments. Similar analyses had previously been made for the oxygen-deficient but rapidly deposited sediment of Santa Barbara Basin off southern California (Degens, Prashnowsky, Emery, and Pimenta, 1961) and for the oxygenated but less rapidly deposited sediment of the San Diego Trough (Degens, Emery, and Reuter, 1963). The concentrations of amino acids in Oyster Pond are greater than those of the Santa Barbara Basin. Concentrations of arginine, lysine, alanine, glycine, leucine, proline, and valine are approximately the same as those for the San Diego Trough. However, the aromatic (phenylalanine and tyrosine) and especially the acidic (aspartic acid and glutamic acid) forms are many times greater in Oyster Pond than in either basin. The significance of these similarities and dissimilarities must remain unknown until the general factors which control the abundance of amino acids in sediments are better understood.

The nitrogen that is incorporated in the amino acids and amino sugars totals only 4.6 and 8.9% of the total Kjeldahl nitrogen (Table 3, Fig. 11), which is several times greater than in the marine basin sediments. Unknown for the pond as well as the marine basins is the form in which most of the nitrogen is present. In both environments nitrogen as ammonia is even less abundant than nitrogen in the form of amino acids.

GASES

The odor of hydrogen sulfide was noted in every sample from the pond floor, whether of silt or sand, and whether the sediment was gray, brown or, black. Hydrogen sulfide also was usually present in the bottom 1 or 2 meters of water within the southern basin where it was trapped in a high-salinity puddle of sea water beneath ordinary pond water. Because of its high solubility, the hydrogen sulfide is in dissolved, not gaseous, form.

Any disturbance of the bottom commonly releases bubbles of gas that rise to the surface. Invariably clouds of bubbles were noted when the bottom sampler was lifted from organic silts, but few or no bubbles came from areas of sand bottom. Measurements by Kanwisher (1962) in the somewhat similar but more saline Eel Pond revealed that gas bubbles like those in Oyster Pond average 50 to 80% methane and that free oxygen is not present in the bottom sediments. In Oyster Pond the gas also is largely methane; a 100-ml sample of the gas collected in a submerged water-filled bottle and funnel burned with a steady blue flame.

During many periods of calm, the glassy surface above the northern basin of the pond is continuously dimpled and ringed by small ripples. The interruptions of the glassy surface are too continuous and widespread to be made by fish, and closer inspection shows them to be caused by the rising and bursting at the surface of bubbles. Counts of bubbles in areas estimated at 10 square meters were made for 10-minute periods at intervals of a few days. These counts revealed that bubbling does not occur during winter, but it begins only about the middle of April when the water warms to about 10°C. By June, when the water reaches about 15°C, the rate was found to be about 4 bubbles per square meter per minute.

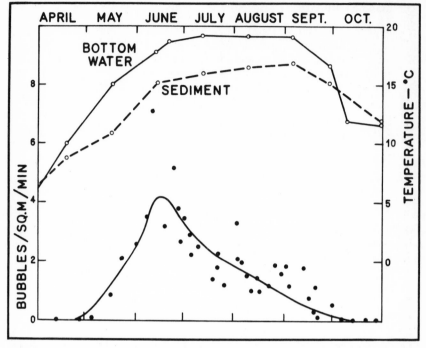

Fig. 14. Rate of escape of gas (methane) bubbles from the northern basin during 1964. Note that the peak rate corresponds with the end of the period of rapid warming of bottom sediments in early summer

If the water is saturated with the methane (9 ml per liter at 20° C), the rate of release at the surface must equal the rate of production at the bottom. The average rate throughout the year is probably about 0.8 bubble per square meter per minute. (Fig. 14). Total production must then be about 14 liters per square meter per year, or 10 gm per square meter per year if all of the gas is methane. The 7.5 gm of carbon in the methane probably amounts to less than 1 % of the annual production of carbon in aqueous plants plus the annual in-fall of carbon in leaves and other debris from the surrounding land, because the annual production of carbon must be at least 400 gm per square meter per year on the basis of a comparison with the productivity of comparable marine waters. Most of the carbon must be released as carbon dioxide or it remains in the bottom sediments in the form of partly altered organic matter. If the methane comes only from the top 20 cm of sediment having an assumed water content of 90 % by wet weight, the rate of escape is about 0.0018 ml per gram dry weight of sediment per day. This is similar to the 0.0024 ml per day of methane released per gram of paddy soil in incubation experiments at 15° C by Koyama (1963).

SUBSURFACE

In February 1945 Deevey (1948) made two borings of the sediments of Oyster Pond using a Davis peat borer lowered through a hole in the ice cover. His OP1 (Fig. 15) was about 20 meters southeast of sample 9 (Fig. 9) and his OP2 was approximately at the center of the triangle formed by samples 3, 4, and 5. Samples at 1-foot intervals in both holes were examined for diatoms to determine the general salinity of the environment of deposition and for pollen to learn the changing forest composition.

Hole OP1 in 3.4 meters of water penetrated 2.4 meters of brackish-water sediment and ended in a drowned forest now 5.8 meters below lake level. Hole OP2 was north of the 2.5-meter sill (2.3-meter, according to Deevey) between the two present basins of Oyster Pond. It was drilled in 4.6 meters of water through 13.4 meters of sediment. The log (Fig. 15) shows that the top 5.5 meters consisted of brackish-water organic sediments and the bottom 7.9 meters was fresh-water organic sediment resting atop inorganic clay. The

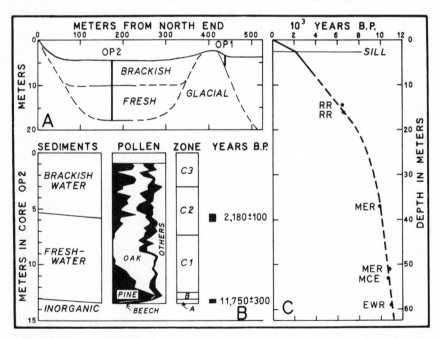

Fig. 15. Stages of filling of the northern basin of Oyster Pond. A. Cross-section of northern basin, its sill, and the adjacent part of the middle basin, according to data from two borings made by Deevey (1948). B. Log of boring OP2 in the northern basin showing past salinity (from diatoms), frequency of chief groups of pollen, pollen zones, and radiocarbon dates (Minze Stuiver—Yale University, personal communication of 20 April 1965). C. Sea level rise curve for the region from solid line (many dates from Barnstable salt marsh—Redfield and Rubin, 1962) and separate points (RR = Redfield and Rubin, 1962; MER = Merrill, Emery, and Rubin, 1965; MCE = Medcof, Clarke, and Erskine, 1965; EWR = Emery, Wigley, and Rubin, 1965).

pollen sequence is normal for the region according to Deevey, with zone A—spruce-fir, B—pine, C1—oak-hemlock, C2—a hickory maximum, and C3—a rise of hemlock and fall of oak, hickory and beech. Only the percentages of pine, oak, and beech are shown separately in Fig. 15.

The salinity sequence based upon diatoms in both holes supports the view that soon after the glacial ice melted and left the kettle of the northern basin, a fresh-water lake occupied the basin. As the sea level rose during the postglacial time the sea water first occupied the southern and middle basins of Oyster Pond. When it rose high enough to spill through the 2.5 meter sill between OP1 and OP2, it filled the northern basin and has remained subsequently (Fig. 15, A). Radiocarbon dates for the bottom of both holes and for the transition from fresh-water to brackish-water sediment in OP2 were desirable, and Deevey and Minze Stuiver kindly make the determinations. The date at the bottom of the fresh-water sediment in OP2 was $11,750\pm300$ years before 1950 (number Y-1459). This is a minimum date for the melting of the Buzzards Bay glacier and it fits well with other dates obtained elsewhere in New England in similar environments: 13,500 in Connecticut (Bloom, 1963), 12,700 at Martha's Vineyard (Rubin and Alexander, 1960; Ogden, 1963), 12,300 at Boston (Kaye and Barghoorn, 1964), and 10,200 at Portland, Maine (Bloom, 1963).

At the date when the first fresh-water sediment was deposited in the. northern basin, the sea level was more than 60 meters below the present level (Fig. 15, C). At that time Vineyard Sound contained no sea water, and in fact the closest ocean shore was about 80 km east of Oyster Pond. The sea gradually rose, filling Vineyard Sound, the southern and middle basins of Oyster Pond and reached the level of -5.7 meters at the date of 3429 ± 120 years ago (number Y-1663). Finally, sea water spilled over the sill into the northern basin. The radiocarbon date of the change to brackish-water sediments at OP2 was found to be 2180 ± 100 years ago (number Y-1458). According to sea-level data derived from the Barnstable salt marsh by Redfield and Rubin (1962), at this date the sea level was about 2.3 meters below the present mean high water level. Since the base level for the pond is 14 cm above mean high water (50 cm above mean low water) in Vineyard Sound, the sill must have been $2.30+0.14$ or 2.44 meters below the present pond level. The present depth of the basin sill is about 2.5 meters, a close check, considering the fact that storm waves could cross the sill from a sea level somewhat lower than the sill.

Another hole was drilled through the ice cover by the author, A. C. Redfield, and many volunteers on 13 January 1968. The equipment was a peat borer capable of collecting piston cores, each 1 foot long, at successively greater depths. Eighteen consecutive cores reached a depth of 5.95 meters beneath a water depth of 6.5 meters at the position of sample 18 of Fig. 9. The core consisted of organic silt (about 10% organic carbon) with layers of sand 0.2 to 2.0 cm thick (shown by dots on Fig. 16). Marine diatoms were present throughout the core. The water content decreases at depth, with irregularities probably corresponding to variations in the content of organic matter. A

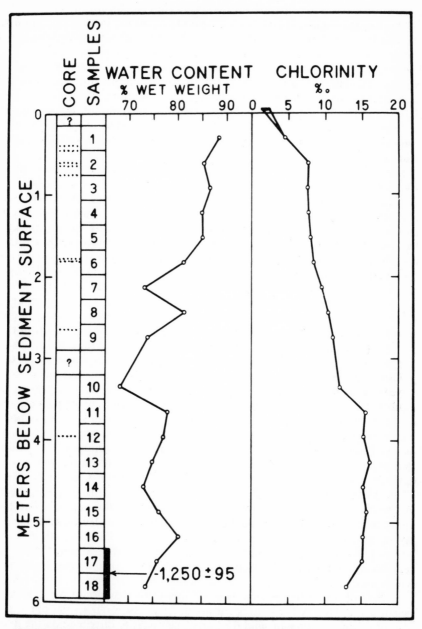

Fig. 16. Stages of filling of the southern basin of Oyster Pond, based upon a core from near the site of surface sample 18 (Fig. 9). The diagram shows the depths of sand layers separated by gray organic silt, and the core sample numbers for which the water content and and chlorinity of interstitial waters were measured by Susan Kadar.

radiocarbon age determination was made by Isotopes Incorporated (number I-3289) for the organic carbon in a 2-foot section at the bottom of the core (5.34 to 5.95 meters in the sediment). The result was 1250±95 years before the present for a point 5.65 meters below the sediment surface, 12.15 meters below mean pond level, and 11.65 meters below mean low water of the open Vineyard Sound. When the core is adjusted to a uniform water content to account for greater compaction at depth and assuming a uniform rate of deposition of solid sediment throughout the core, the dates of deposition for materials now at 1-meter depth intervals were computed to be as follows: 0 m—0, 1 m—120, 2 m—300, 3 m—540, 4 m—820, 5 m—1100, and 6 m—1330 years ago.

The interstitial waters trapped in the sediment that was deposited 1100 to 700 years ago (5.0 to 3.5 meters of core) had a chlorinity of 16‰, nearly as great as that of the present Vineyard Sound (see Table 4). Afterward the chlorinity gradually decreased. By 200 years ago (1.5 meters) when the oysters disappeared, according to records of the town, the chlorinity had dropped to less than 8‰. Subsequently, the drop in chlorinity continued, with a sharp drop beginning about 70 years ago (0.6 meter) (probably corresponding with the building of the railroad embankment) to only 1–2‰, as shown by Fig. 16 and 26. The upward increase in chlorinity suggested by the bottom few points of Fig. 16 may not be real because the date (1100 to 1300 years ago) was too recent to mark the transition from fresh water to sea water; conceivably, however, this trend is due to downward diffusion of salts from the marine phase into the earlier and lower fresh-water phase of the pond.

The sand layers in the core probably represent material washed into the pond by hurricane waves. A sand layer that includes cinders and bits of coal washed from the railroad embankment by the 1938 hurricane is present in most surface samples from near the core site. It was not sampled by the corer owing to inability of the instrument to retain the top fluidlike layer of sediment. The sands that were sampled, however, can be approximately dated using the same assumptions about compaction and uniformity of deposition that were applied to the discussion of chlorinity of the interstitial water. The dates for the nine sand layers shown by Fig. 16 are 1930, 1920, 1905, 1895, 1780, 1510, 1500, 1290, and 960 A.D., respectively. This range is much greater than that permitted by historical records (Ludlum, 1963). The accuracy of dating is probably no greater than about 50 years for the earlier sand layers; nevertheless, the figures suggest that hurricanes large enough to leave a record as a sand layer appear to be increasing in frequency during the period represented by the core. Inspection of Fig. 16 shows that the period during which sand layers were deposited corresponds with the period of decreasing chlorinity of interstitial waters. The building of the baymouth bar evidently began about 1100 A.D., cutting off access of ocean water to the pond and also providing a source of sand for hurricane waves to distribute on the floor of the southern basin.

Radiocarbon dates also provide information on the rate of deposition of the sediments. These rates are 78 cm/1000 years for the fresh-water sediments and

260 cm/1000 years for the brackish-water ones in the northern basin, and 360 cm/1000 years for brackish-water ones in the southern basin. The more than three times greater rate for the brackish-water than for the fresh-water sediments is probably due not only to lesser compaction (higher water content) near the surface of the bottom, but it must mean a significantly faster contribution during the past few thousand years than earlier. If the water content averages 75% by wet weight at depth, a reasonable average of 340 cm/1000 years corresponds to 100 gm per square centimeter per 1000 years, or 100 mg per square centimeter per year.

6 Water

GENERAL RELATIONSHIP TO CLIMATE

Water in Oyster Pond is controlled chiefly by the local weather. Long-term meteorological data are presented by Fig. 17. Since there was no nearby weather station prior to 1964, the data had to be obtained from various private and public sources, but all of these sources have records of 15 years or longer.

Air temperature reported by Fig. 17 comes from measurements taken for 20 years by Charles Packard at Woods Hole 0.1 km from the shore. Other temperatures were measured by W. G. Metcalf for 10 years at his home in Falmouth; because of its location 1.5 km inland, the mean summer temperatures at Falmouth are about 0.5°C higher than those at Woods Hole and the winter ones are about 0.3°C lower. Similarly, a 50-year Weather Bureau record at Nantucket Island exhibits mean summer values about 1.0°C lower and winter ones about 0.2°C higher than those at Woods Hole because of the more marine environment of the island 45 km offshore.

Sea-water temperatures at Woods Hole lag behind air temperatures a week or two on the average so that the water is cooler than the air during spring, and warmer during late summer and fall. Perhaps the fact that the water is warmer than the air during fall is partly responsible for greater evaporation then, as reflected by higher salinities in the sea water during late summer and fall than at other times of year. However, it should be noted that slightly lower precipitation also characterizes that period of the year.

Slightly clearer skies are typical of the fall months, corresponding to a shift of the wind from southeasterly between May and October to northwesterly during November to April. The summer months also are characteristically ones of low wind speed (about 18 km per hour), in contrast to the winter months of higher wind speeds (about 24 km per hour). Highest humidities occur during the summer when mean values are about 90% during the night and about 72% during the early afternoon. During the winter these humidities average about 80 and 69%, respectively. The seasonal change of humidity evidently is caused by the seasonal change of wind from sea to land sources. The diurnal difference, shown by Fig. 17, is probably the result of higher air temperatures in the afternoon than at night.

The temperature and precipitation regimens require that the area be classified as mesothermal, constantly moist, or *Cfb*, according to the Köppen classification of climates.

Like most of the Atlantic coast of the United States, the area of Cape Cod is subject to hurricanes during the fall months, notable recent ones having occurred on 21 September 1938, 14 September 1944, and 31 August 1954 (Gray, 1944; Redfield and Miller, 1957; Galtsoff, 1962). Each of these hurricanes affected Oyster Pond by the flow of sea water across the baymouth bar, by shoreline erosion, and by introduction of large quantities of vegetation and man-made debris.

30

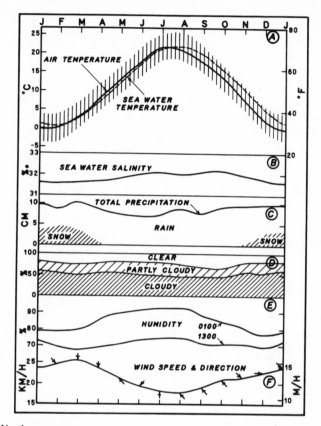

Fig. 17. Weather summary.

A. *Temperature*. Solid line is monthly mean of daily mean air temperatures for 1943–62 for   north side of Marine Biological Laboratory. (Data from Charles Packard.) Vertical hatching—monthly mean of daily maximum and minimum temperatures; same source as above. Dashed line—monthly mean of daily ocean water temperatures for 1944–62 at the Pier of the Woods Hole Oceanographic Institution. [Data from Coast and Geodetic Survey (1953, 1960), Day (1959, 1963), and unpublished material in files of Woods Hole Oceanographic Institution.]

B. *Salinity*. Monthly mean of daily measurements of salinity for 1944–58 computed from measurements of density on samples of surface sea water from pier at Woods Hole Oceanographic Institution. (From Coast and Geodetic Survey, 1953, 1957.)

C. *Precipitation*. Monthly mean of daily mean measurements of total precipitation for 1911–61 at Nantucket Island. (From Weather Bureau, 1961.) Snowfall for 1947–61 is indicated as water equivalent on an assumed ratio of 6 to 1.

D. *Cloudiness*. Monthly mean percentage of cloudy, partly cloudy, and clear days (sunrise to sunset) for 1947–61 at Nantucket Island. (From Weather Bureau, 1961.)

E. *Humidity*. Monthly mean of daily measurements of percentage humidity for 0.00 and 1300 hours; based upon data for 1947–61 at Nantucket Island. (From Weather Bureau, 1961.)

F. *Winds*. Monthly mean of hourly mean wind speed for 1947–61 at Nantucket Island. (From Weather Bureau, 1961.) Arrows indicate the prevailing direction of wind where north is top of graph.

TEMPERATURE

Measurements of weekly maximum and minimum air and water temperatures made at the Emery pier at the north end of the pond are shown by Figs. 18, 19, 20, and 21. For comparison, the weekly range of individual daily measurements of sea-water temperature at Woods Hole Oceanographic Institution is included. The results show that the weekly range of pond-water temperature is 10 to 40% of that of the air. The midpoint of the range for the water is generally higher than the midpoint for the air, possibly because of a greenhouse effect. The temperature of the pond water is, of course, never lower than 0°C, and temperatures lower than 1.0° C were restricted to the period of ice cover. Comparison of surface temperatures of the pond and of the ocean during the spring and fall reveals a lag in the ocean temperature of 2 to 6 weeks, resulting probably from the larger mass of ocean water and to its circulation.

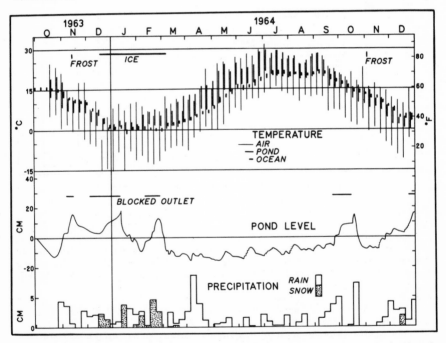

Fig. 18. Measurements for 1963 and 1964 at the Emery pier (Fig. 22) near the landward end of the pond. Weekly maximum–minimum air temperatures are from a thermometer placed about 1 meter above the pond level; weekly maximum–minimum water temperatures are from another thermometer 15 to 40 cm below the water surface. The pond level was generalized from the recording of an automatic water-level recorder. Precipitation was measured with a rain gauge on the pier.

The areal pattern of surface water temperature throughout the pond is illustrated by two surveys, one conducted in October and the other in May

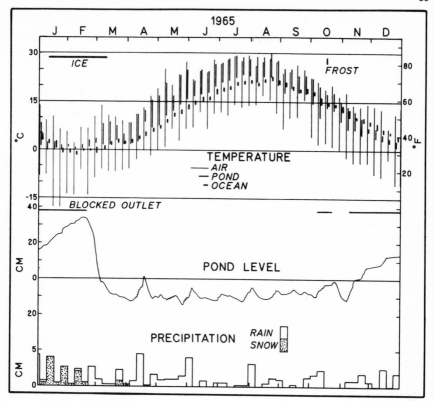

Fig. 19. Measurements for 1965 at the Emery pier. See Fig. 18 for description.

(Fig. 22). Both exhibit a general increase in temperature from the seaward end to the landward end of the pond. Measurements at 4-week intervals at positions over the two basins at opposite ends of the pond indicate that the surface temperature averages 0.4°C higher at the north end than at the south during the spring and summer, and it averages about 0.1°C lower at the south during the fall and winter.

The annual variation of properties of the subsurface waters of the pond was determined by measurements of temperature and chlorinity on samples at 1-meter depth increments at 4-week intervals near the middle of both the northern and the southern basins (Figs. 23 and 24). All the water samples were collected in a lead-weighted bottle lowered to the desired depth by a nylon cord knotted at 1-meter intervals. After allowing a minute for the bottle to come to the temperature of the water surrounding it, the cord was jerked, thereby pulling out a rubber stopper to permit the bottle to fill. Immediately upon recovery of the bottle, a thermometer was inserted and the temperature noted. About 250 ml of the water was transferred to a storage bottle for later measurement of chlorinity.

34

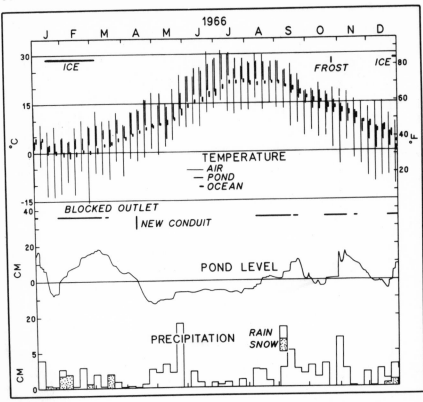

Fig. 20. Measurements for 1966 at the Emery pier. See Fig. 18 for description.

   The temperature data of Figs. 23 and 24 reveal nearly isothermal conditions in the top 4 meters throughout most of the year, a result of wind mixing. A thermocline is present in the northern basin only during the summer, and there is no halocline. Conditions in the southern basin are more complex, owing to the presence of an isolated puddle of more saline water that is always deeper than 4 meters. Because of the high density produced by the salt, the temperature of this water was found to be somewhat independent of that of the overlying water. Temperatures became isothermal to the bottom at about 4°C during two periods of overturn about 30 November 1963 and 9 March 1964, but overturn failed to occur again until 29 April 1967 during 2 days of very strong northeasterly winds.

ICE

Cooling of the air below the temperature of the pond water initiates morning steaming of the pond during early October, and the first frost comes about a month later. In December or January, after several days of air temperature lower than about 25°C (Figs. 18, 19, 20, and 21), the pond surface takes on a heavy, almost oily appearance. The next day it is largely covered with ice except near the shores. During the winters of 1962–63, 1963–64, 1964–65, 1965–66, and 1967–68 the ice reached a maximum thickness of about 25 cm, but during the winter of 1966–67 it was only about 5 cm because of the unusually mild weather.

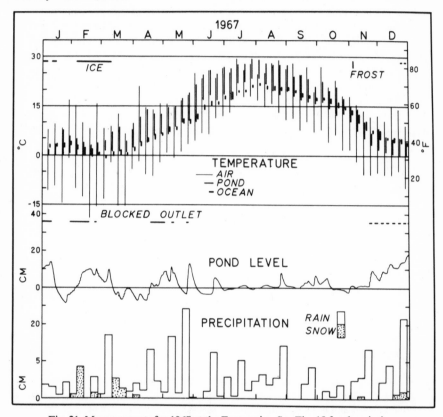

Fig. 21. Measurements for 1967 at the Emery pier. See Fig. 18 for description.

Local variations in ice thickness depend upon the inclusion of snow and rain at the top as well as upon new freezing or melting at the bottom. As a result, the ice is generally well stratified in layers of varying color and hardness. Color stratification is particularly obvious after loading by snow has caused the ice to sink, permitting the brownish pond water to extrude atop the ice in the form of small fountains [as described by Woodcock (1965)]. Irregular raylike channels carry the pond water atop the ice for several meters from the fountains.

Characteristically, thin ice or even open water borders the west- and south-facing shores to a width of 1 to 10 meters. This open zone is attributed to warming of these shores by afternoon sunlight and by conduction of heat from the shores. That the open water is not due only to inflow of ground water is shown by the presence of open water at projecting points. Shrinkage of thick ice during exceptionally cold days produces tension cracks, many of which can be traced entirely across the pond. One of the clearest cracks occurs each year directly off the projecting point that separates the northern basin from the main part of the pond. These cracks part and others form when the ice cover is disturbed by strong winds or by rapid lowering of the water level when the outlet is opened. At these times the movements are accompanied by loud noises almost like pistol shots. In many areas ice shove against the shore is due to freezing of new ice in open cracks, followed by expansion of the ice upon warming. Ice shove along the shores of Oyster Pond is minor and appears to be due more to wind stress than to expansion of the ice. Signs of a general break up of the ice occur for several weeks, but the actual disappearance of the ice is usually sudden and takes place about the middle of March.

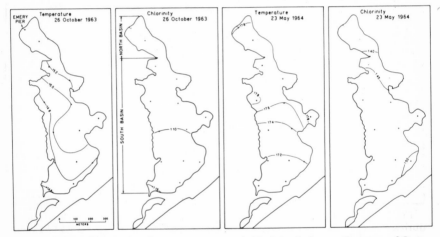

Fig. 22. Distribution of surface temperature and chlorinity during areal surveys of Oyster Pond in October and in May. Transparencies by Secchi disk ranged between 90 and 105 cm with no apparent pattern.

When the ice cover forms, the underlying water is nearly isothermal at 0°C (Figs. 23 and 24). About a month later the water beneath the ice warms to 2°C, and by early March the water is about 4°C. It is evident that once an ice cover is present it serves as an insulating surface that allows the accumulation of heat from conduction through the bottom, from the inflow of ground water, and from biological activities. The ice also prevents stirring of the underlying water by wind. Accordingly, the ice serves as its own executioner by permitting the underlying water to store heat until its temperature is sufficiently high to melt the ice.

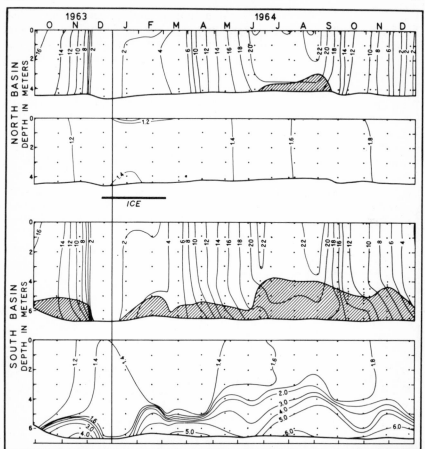

Fig. 23. Results of serial measurements of water properties made at 4-week intervals during 1963 and 1964. *Top panels*—Isotherms (above) and isochlors (below) near the center of the northern basin (Station 3 of Fig. 9). *Bottom panels*—Isotherms (above) and isochlors (below) in the deepest area of the southern basin (station 18 of Fig. 9). Isotherms are in °C, isochlors are chlorinity in parts per thousand. Cross-hatching indicates the presence of hydrogen sulfide in the water.

CHLORINITY AND SALINITY

Analyses for chlorinity were made by titration with silver nitrate against a conductometric end point. Repeated standardization against Copenhagen normal sea water indicates an accuracy of about 0.02 ‰. Total salinity was measured on a separate aliquot by electrical conductivity, with an estimated accuracy of 0.25 ‰

During two areal surveys (Fig. 22) water samples were collected at about 10 cm depths at 14 stations throughout the pond. The analyses show a general

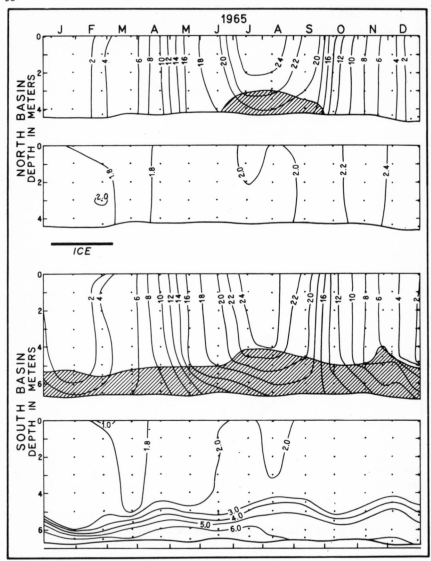

Fig. 24. Measurements of water properties during 1965. See Fig. 23 for description.

decrease of chlorinity from the seaward to the landward end of the pond. The average difference between chlorinities above the northern and the southern basins based upon 30 pairs of stations at 4-week intervals (Figs. 23, 24, and 25) is 0.05 ‰, with lower chlorinities at the north. The higher chlorinities at the south must be due to occasional incursions of sea water from the adjacent Vineyard Sound.

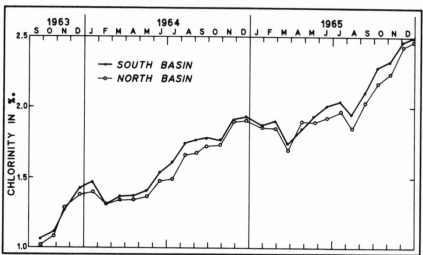

Fig. 25. Chlorinities of the top 4-meters of water above the northern and the southern basins measured for several years mostly at 4-week intervals. Each point is based upon four measurements at 1, 2, 3, and 4 meters depth, unless the 4-meter value was influenced by the sharp halocline in the southern basin, when the value at the surface was substituted for the 4-meter one. Note the general rise of chlorinity during the period of measurement.

The 4-week surveys show the water of the northern basin to be nearly uniform in chlorinity from top to bottom, except for low chlorinities at the very surface in January and February that were produced by partial melting of the ice cover (Figs. 23 and 24). At the southern basin the chlorinity was also found to be nearly uniform from the surface to depths of 4 meters. Below 5 meters, however, the water commonly has chlorinities of 3 to 6‰, in contrast to 1 to 2‰ in the overlying water. This saline bottom water is quite evidently the result of inflows of sea water through the shallow and narrow connection with Vineyard Sound at high spring tides. During the periods of overturn the saline bottom water becomes thoroughly mixed with the overlying water, eliminating the halocline and raising the chlorinity in the top 4 meters. The overturn of 9 March 1964 had less effect upon bottom water than the previous fall overturn probably because the temperature rise through 4°C (temperature of maximum density for fresh water) was not accompanied by strong winds as was the fall overturn.

The only pre-1963 measurement of record appears to be one by Deevey (1948), who reported a surface salinity of 1.7‰. This salinity corresponds with a chlorinity of about 1.1‰, approximately the same as that noted in 1963 (Fig. 26). The rapid rise of chlorinity in the mixed layer (between the surface and 4 meters) probably owes its origin to the sharp decrease in the annual total precipitation for the years 1964–1966. The precipitation for 1965 was the lowest since records began in 1847 at Nantucket Island. Low precipitation provides little fresh water for flushing out sea water that enters the pond during high spring tides.

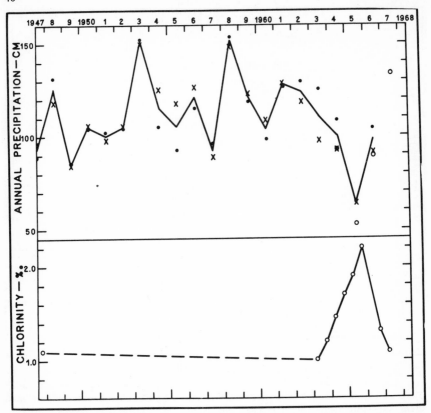

Fig. 26. Total annual precipitation at Nantucket Island (dots), Hatchville near Falmouth (crosses), and the Emery pier (circles). The line connects the average values for Nantucket and Hatchville. Note the high chlorinity in Oyster Pond during recent years of low precipitation, particularly for 1965.

Oceanographers commonly plot temperature against salinity to depict a vertical column of ocean water and to show the density stability with depth. Similar plots were constructed for the water of the southern basin for alternate sets of the measurements given by Figs. 23 and 24. These plots (Fig. 27) show temperature versus chlorinity in comparison with a grid of σ_t lines $[\sigma_t = (\rho_t - 1.000) \times 1000]$, where ρ_t is the density of the water at the *in situ* temperature. The plots exhibit a progressive change that for most of the year is caused only by a temperature increase or decrease in the whole water column. After the fall overturn, the loss of salinity stratification caused the points for the whole water column in December to be nearly superimposed. The plots also show that cooling alone cannot cause the surface water to become denser than the more saline bottom water; wind stirring is essential for producing iso-density water throughout the whole water column.

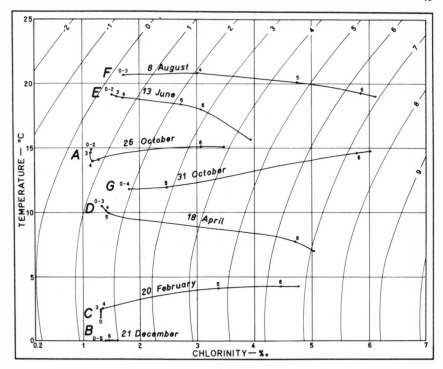

Fig. 27. Temperature-chlorinity diagram showing temperature plotted against chlorinity at 8-week intervals between 26 October 1963 and 29 October 1964 for the southern basin. The curved grid presents σ_t lines. Each of the seven plots (lettered A to G in chronological order) has depths in meters indicated by small numerals.

A comparison of chlorinity and salinity measured for 106 samples of pond water shows a clear-cut dependence of the two values (Fig. 28). The relationship is nearly the same as that for the mixture of sea water with the fresh water of the Baltic Sea, from which the formula, Sal=1.805 Cl+0.03, was derived (Sverdrup, Johnson, and Fleming, 1942, pp. 51, 59). The empirical formula from the data of Fig. 28 is Sal=1.85 Cl−0.3; this suggests the presence of an excess amount of chlorine, possibly from septic tank leakage. The main conclusion is that the pond water is a mixture of ocean water and variable amounts of nearly ion-free water from direct precipitation, runoff, and ground water.

CHEMICAL COMPOSITION

Chemical analyses were made by the U.S. Geological Survey for four samples of pond water, one of the ocean water about 15 meters offshore (at the middle of the shore zone of Fig. 6), and one of ground water about 10 meters north of the head of the pond (north of the Emery pier). All samples were collected during the late spring of 1964. The results are presented in Table 4.

TABLE 4
Chemical Composition (ppm) of Natural Waters

Ion	Ocean, general average[1]	Ocean at The Groin, 0.1 m 21 March	South Basin, 6.3 m 21 March	South Basin, 6.2 m 23 May	South Basin, 0.1 m 21 March	North Basin, 0.1 m 21 March	Ground water, 23 May
Calcium	362	370	109	88	34	33	3.2
Magnesium	1155	1160	347	279	97	94	2.4
Sodium	9580	9380	2650	2170	762	740	18.0
Potassium	344	381	111	92	29	28	2.7
Bicarbonate	127	130	56	57	32	32	—
Sulfate	2400	2340	663	529	190	184	16.0
Chloride	17,200	17,200	4870	3940	1380	1340	36.0
Silicate		0.1	4.4	4.0	1.2	1.2	16.0

[1]Sverdrup, Johnson, and Fleming (1942, p. 176) adjusted to 17.200‰ chlorinity.

The analyses for ocean water agree within 3 % of average values for the ocean (Sverdrup, Johnson, and Fleming, 1942, p. 176), when the latter are adjusted to the same chlorinity. Most ions in the samples of pond water have ratios to chloride nearly identical with the ratios in ocean water. Only the

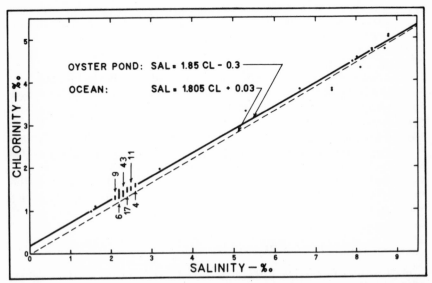

Fig. 28. Relationship of chlorinity and salinity in samples of pond water as compared with the relationship in sea water.

ratio of bicarbonate to chloride exhibits a major departure, being about three times greater in the samples of the most dilute pond waters than in ocean water. These relatively high concentrations of bicarbonate are due probably to carbon dioxide released from the abundant organic matter in the bottom sediments. The ratio of sulfate to chloride is slightly lower at depth than in the surface water, indicating that less than 2% of the sulfate had been reduced to sulfide and lost by upward diffusion.

If we assume that the pond water consists of ocean water diluted with rain water having zero salt content, we find that the sample of surface water from the northern basin contained 7.8% ocean water, and that from the southern basin had 8.0%. The two samples of bottom water from the southern basin contained 28.9 and 23.5% ocean water, respectively. The ground water contains such a low concentration of salts that computations based upon dilution of ocean water by ground water reduce the percentages of ocean water in Oyster Pond by only half a percentage point. It is evident that the water of Oyster Pond is a simple dilution of ocean water. The dilutent consists of direct infall of rain or snow, subaqueous inflow of ground water having a very low ion content, plus some inflow of tap water largely through cesspools. The chlorinity of the tap water is only about 11 ppm, which is even lower than that of the ground water.

DISSOLVED ORGANIC COMPOUNDS

The water of Oyster Pond contains much higher concentrations of dissolved organic matter than the open ocean. Measurements by D. W. Menzel of water samples collected at 3-hour intervals during a day in June 1964 exhibited values that fluctuated between 5 and 10 mg of carbon per liter, with no definite diurnal cycle. Additional samples from the water surface and from 50 cm above the bottom at stations 3 and 18 (Fig. 9), and at the conduits beneath the highway and the railroad were collected on 17 May 1965. Concentrations ranged between 7.5 and 9.5 mg of carbon per liter. Because such concentrations are nearly 100 times the range in most ocean water for which Menzel's instruments are calibrated (Menzel and Vaccaro, 1964), the samples had to be diluted with distilled water, and the values are to be considered accurate to only $\pm20\%$.

Analyses were made by Walsh (1965b, 1966) for two components of the dissolved organic matter: carbohydrate and chlorophyll a. The dissolved carbohydrate exhibits a diurnal cycle (Fig. 32) with highest values during the time of day that photosynthesis is greatest, as though during daytime it was produced by algae and at night it was used as an energy source by various organisms. It has a similar annual cycle (Fig. 29), with highest surface values during the spring. Even greater values occurred in the bottom waters after a July–August bloom of *Chlorobium*.

Surface and mid-depth values of chlorophyll a presented a general inverse relationship to dissolved carbohydrate for both diurnal measurements and annual ones, except during the *Chlorobium* bloom of July and August, when

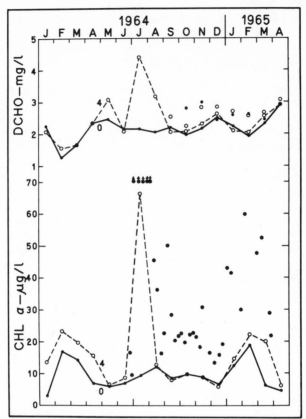

Fig. 29. Dissolved organic compounds in the water over the northern basin of Oyster Pond. *Carbohydrate:* solid line with dots—morning values in surface water; dashed line with circles—morning values in bottom water (4 meters); isolated dots and circles—afternoon values in surface and bottom waters, respectively. (Data from Walsh, 1966.) *Chlorophyll a:* solid line with dots—morning values in surface water; dashed line with circles—morning values in bottom water (4 meters). (Data from Walsh, 1966.) Isolated large dots are morning values for composite integrated water samples from bottom to surface of the pond. (Analyses by C. S. Yentsch.)

both compounds were abundant (Fig. 29). Measurements at water depths below the zone of photosynthesis yielded greater concentrations than at the surface, possibly a result of the method of analysis that was unable to discriminate between chlorophyll *a* at the surface and phaeophytin (and other green pigments). The latter are intermediate decomposition products of chlorophyll *a* and accumulate in bottom waters and sediments.

In addition to Walsh's measurements at discrete depths in the pond, C. S. Yentsch made additional analyses on composite integrated samples from the bottom to the surface of the northern basin (Fig. 29). These values are higher than Walsh's probably because the analyses were made after the walls of suspended cells were broken by grinding (Yentsch and Menzel, 1963).

OXIDATION-REDUCTION POTENTIAL AND pH

Water samples collected during a regular survey in the summer of 1964 were tested for pH and Eh using a Beckman Expanded Scale meter standardized for each parameter. The results (Fig. 30) show that the pH of the water in the pond, lower than the usual 8.0 to 8.3 of sea water, ranged between 6.5 and 7.9. Highest pH occurred at about 1 meter, probably in response to the removal of carbon dioxide by the actively growing phytoplankton. About 10 cm below the surface of the sediment the pH dropped to its lowest value, possibly the result of excess carbon dioxide produced by decomposition of organic matter.

The oxidation-reduction potential (referred to the hydrogen electrode) exhibited only a narrow range of +400 to +428 mV throughout the top 6 meters of water. Within the saline bottom water of the southern basin, where hydrogen sulfide was present, the Eh dropped to −135 mV. The bottom sediment of the southern basin was −140 mV and that of the northern basin −107 mV. Such negative values were fully expected in view of the strong

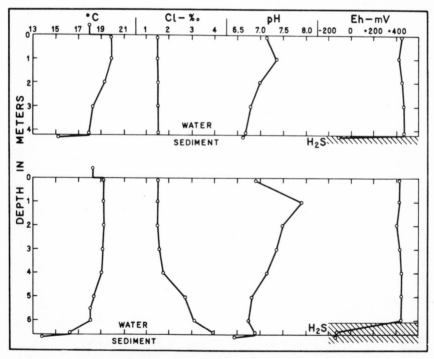

Fig. 30. Measurements at the northern basin (top) and the southern basin showing the relationship of pH and Eh to temperature and chlorinity of the water and bottom sediment. Data are for 0900 to 1030 on 13 June 1964.

odor of volatile hydrogen sulfide (Baas Becking, Kaplan, and Moore, 1960), and doubtlessly they characterize the floor of almost the entire pond.

Monthly measurements of pH and Eh in the waters of both basins exhibited annual cycles (Fig. 31). Smoothest cycles occurred in the surface waters, with the pH rising from values between 7.0 and 7.5 during winter to 8.5 during summer; evidently, this was an effect of biological use of bicarbonate ion during the spring and summer. Eh ranged generally between +400 and +250 mV, with lowest values during the summer. The pH at depth was approximately the same as that near the surface except during the summer, when it failed to increase because of negligible photosynthetic activity at depth. Eh near the bottom of the northern basin was similar to that near the surface except during summer, when negative values were associated with the hydrogen sulfide below the thermocline (Fig. 23). Values of Eh beneath the strong halocline at the bottom of the southern basin were as low as −127 mV except during the overturn of early spring.

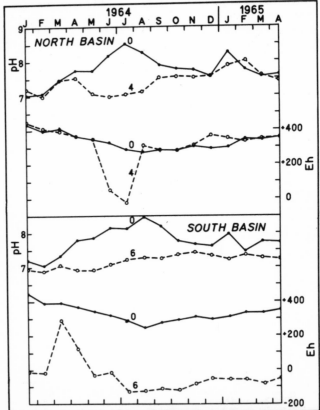

Fig. 31. Annual variation of pH and Eh in the water near the surface and near the bottom of both basins. The depth in meters of the samples is given by the numbers 0, 4, and 6. All of these monthly measurements were made by Walsh (1966).

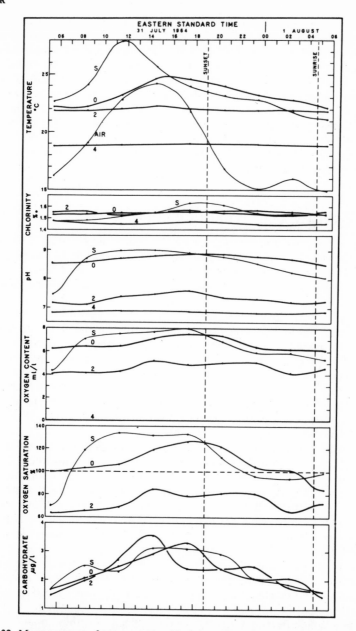

Fig. 32. Measurements of temperature, chlorinity, pH, oxygen, and carbohydrate content at 3-hour intervals throughout a 24-hour period. The symbol S is for data in water 20 cm deep at the Emery pier; 0, 2, and 4 are for data at those depths in meters at the center of the northern basin. All measurements were made cooperatively with G. E. Walsh (Marine Biological Laboratory).

Measurements of pH throughout a 24-hour period reveal a typical increase during the daytime and a decrease at night (Fig. 32). This cycle corresponds to the production of oxygen and use of bicarbonate ion during the daytime by photosynthesis of plants, followed by the use of oxygen and production of bicarbonate by respiration of both plants and animals. The diurnal cycle is most prominent in shallow water where attached plants comprise the bulk of the flora. In the open pond pH undergoes greater variation at the surface than at depth owing to greater photosynthesis near the surface than deeper. The fact that the shore and the surface values of pH range between 9 and 7.5 is to be expected of the oxygen-carbon dioxide system which is buffered by calcium carbonate just as it is in the open sea. However, the values lower than 7 at depth indicate the presence of concentrations of organic acids.

OXYGEN AND HYDROGEN SULFIDE

Analyses of oxygen content of the waters at several depths were made during late summer using the Winkler method. The results (Fig. 32) show a range from 0 in the bottom water, where hydrogen sulfide was present, to a maximum of 8 ml per liter at the surface. Measurements soon after an overturn would have shown more oxygen at depth; others made during the winter months of low photosynthetic activity would have yielded lower values near the surface. The higher content of oxygen during the daytime than at nighttime is an obvious result of the diurnal cycle of photosynthesis. Of course, respiration by both plants and animals occurs during both day and night. Photosynthesis is so intense that the surface waters become supersaturated with oxygen (to 135%) during much of the daytime and the early part of the night. Losses of oxygen to the air by both gaseous diffusion and escape of bubbles must occur during the daytime in amounts far greater than are returned by diffusion from the air at night.

Hydrogen sulfide was detected by odor in samples of the bottom water of the northern basin during summer months when a thermocline is present; during the rest of the year both the thermocline and the odor are absent (Figs. 23 and 24). Hydrogen sulfide occurs throughout almost the entire year in the saline bottom water of the southern basin, but it is shallowest during the summer months when a thermocline as well as a halocline is present. During the overturn of 29 April 1967 the odor was noted along the leeward shore of the southern part of the pond.

A single set of measurements (Fig. 33) showed an increase in concentration of hydrogen sulfide with depth to more than 70 ml per liter about 10 cm above the bottom. No doubt, the hydrogen sulfide is formed by sulfate-reducing bacteria present in the bottom sediments and water. Usually the top of the hydrogen sulfide-bearing water can be determined to within about 5 cm. The top 5 to 15 cm of the water generally has only a weak or moderate odor and it is milky. Water from greater depth has a strong odor and is darker than the surface water but with no obvious suspended matter. Samples of the deeper water become milky in a few hours, but the milkiness in both kinds of samples

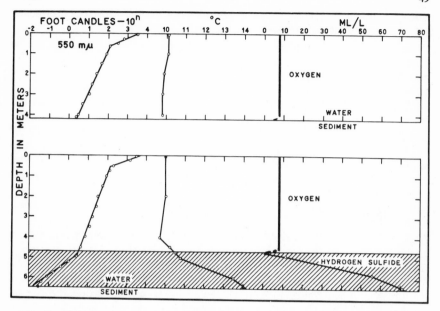

Fig. 33. Light intensity, temperature, and contents of oxygen and hydrogen sulfide in waters of the northern basin (*top*) and the southern basin (*bottom*). Data for the light intensity were measured by J. W. Kanwisher with his meter that is sensitive to only 550 mμ (yellow); data for oxygen were obtained with his *in situ* oxygen meter. Analyses for hydrogen sulfide were made gravimetrically by F. T. Manheim. The cross-hatched area shows the depth range of bottom water having an odor of hydrogen sulfide. All data are for 7 November 1964 except that for hydrogen sulfide, for which samples were collected on 3 November.

disappears in a day or so. The milky appearance is believed due to bacterial precipitation of molecular sulfur from hydrogen sulfide when oxygen is introduced either naturally in the pond or artificially during the collection of water samples. The later clearing of the milkiness is probably due to conversion of the molecular sulfur to sulfate by further bacterial action.

TRANSPARENCY AND COLOR

The transparency of the pond water was measured many times with a Secchi disk, and is expressed as the depth at which a 20-cm white disk disappears from view. During two general surveys (Fig. 22) the transparency varied only between 90 and 105 cm with no apparent pattern of areal distribution. Measurements at 4-week intervals over both basins, however, revealed a systematic seasonal variation. Highest (best) transparencies were noted during the winter through the small holes cut into the ice cover for observation and sampling. Once a measure of 250 cm was obtained, but the average for October to March was 135 cm. During April to September the transparencies ranged down to 85 cm, and they averaged 105 cm. The summer decrease of transparency is a result of intensive growth of phytoplankton; no effect of suspended detrital sediment is evident.

Experiments at photographing the bottom revealed the presence of a turbid layer at depth in both basins. When the unit's flash bulb was fired at depths greater than about 2 meters the flash could not be seen at the surface. No photographs were obtained even during January after an ice cover had had ample time to reduce growth of phytoplankton, inflow of detrital sediment, and stirring of the bottom sediment.

Water samples collected from the bottom meter, particularly in the southern basin, are commonly darker but yet clearer than those of the over-lying water, especially when an odor of hydrogen sulfide is present. Phyto-plankton appear to be absent in the bottom layer of water, and hydrogen sulfide in that layer probably causes precipitation of other particulate materials. Water from the very top of this layer contains a milky precipitate which probably absorbs much of the light that reaches that depth.

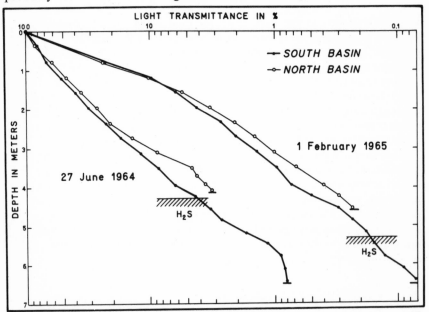

Fig. 34. Relative intensity of ambient light at various depths. Note that the rate of decrease of light intensity decreases in the bottom meter of both basins, indicating the presence of a bottom layer of clearer water. The measurements were made in company with C. S. Yentsch.

Measurements of the intensity of ambient light were made in both basins using two different devices. One meter responds only to yellow light (Fig. 33) and the other to a wide range of wavelengths (Fig. 34). The curves showing the variation of light intensity with depth differ in shape, but the main portions of all of them exhibit a decrease of light intensity amounting to one order of magnitude per 2.5 meters of depth. Two sets of measurements indicate that ambient light at depth was nearly one order of magnitude lower on 1 February 1965 than on 27 June 1964. This difference is probably caused by reflection and absorption of incident light by a 25-cm cover of ice during February.

Color of the pond water was estimated on many occasions by means of Forel color tubes which express color in terms of percentage of yellow in a range from pure yellow to pure blue. In the absence of ice cover, the color above the northern basin generally ranges between 60 and 65% yellow and that above the southern basin is about 50% yellow. The water of the adjacent Vineyard Sound is typically about 30% yellow. The high concentrations of yellow, particularly above the northern basin, probably mean greater concentrations of phytoplankton in the pond.

WAVES AND CURRENTS

Waves are largest in the southern three quarters of Oyster Pond where the pond is widest and most exposed to the wind. The greatest wave height observed between 1962 and 1967 was about 60 cm. In the small protected northern basin the highest waves were about 30 cm, which came through the narrow strait from the south. These waves have produced sufficient turbulence to winnow fine sediment from most of the shores and to leave a residual concentration of sand, gravel, and boulders. During times of hurricanes much higher waves have been reported, but no measurements are available. Their height is attested, however, by the destruction in 1938 of a small cabin on the narrow point which separates north basin from the rest of the pond. In addition, there appears to be a narrow terrace locally present along some of the southward-facing shores about 1.5 meters above the general level of the pond; this terrace may have been eroded by high waves of a hurricane associated with abnormally high water level.

Seiches in lakes have periods that are controlled by the dimensions of the lake, according to the formula (Sverdrup, Johnson, and Fleming, 1942, p. 541)

$$T = \frac{4l}{\sqrt{gh}}$$

where T is the period in seconds, l is the length, and h is the depth. For Oyster Pond l and h are 1050 meters and 3 meters respectively; therefore T is 13 minutes. Available instrumentation has failed to reveal such a seiche, but one may develop if the water should be set in motion by a major atmospheric disturbance such as a hurricane. A hurricane, in addition, can produce an abnormally high water level by pressing sea water against the coast so that some of it spills over the spit into the pond (Redfield and Miller, 1957). Such spillage during the past probably produced several features which appear to be small washover fans on the pond side of the spit, and it transported cinders and beach sand into the deepest part of the pond where they are found in bottom samples.

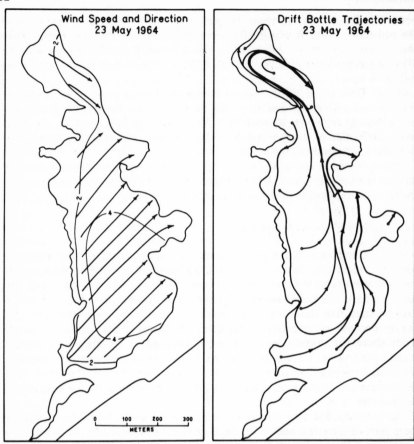

Fig. 35. Wind and surface currents in Oyster Pond during a typical day. Left panel shows wind streamlines and contours of wind speed in meters per second. Right panel shows inferred paths followed by drift bottles. Three bottles were set adrift at each of 16 stations during one morning and they were collected at about the same time the next day.

Currents in Oyster Pond mostly result from wind drag. Other minor currents are associated with the influx of sea water and possibly of ground water, and with the discharge of pond water into the adjacent sound. Measurement of surface currents was accomplished in several ways on 23 May 1964. Three drift bottles were placed at each of 16 stations (14 of which were the same as for the temperature-chlorinity survey of Fig. 22); about 24 hours later they were collected from the shores to which they had drifted. Drift bottles are somewhat unsatisfactory because they reveal only the start and the end of a path; intermediate points must be inferred largely by drawing trajectories which do not cross. The result of the drift bottle study (Fig. 35) reveals a general counterclockwise current in the large southern and middle part of the pond. The long circuitous route designated for the bottles placed just south of the projecting point is admittedly uncertain; however, all three bottles from this station were found close together and associated with the bottles from the southwesternmost station, as indicated. It is notable that most lakes of the northern hemisphere have the same counterclockwise direction of surface currents. Drift bottles in the northern basin had a clockwise movement, with the inferred pattern supported by the finding of two bottles at intermediate points during their periods of drift. Additional support is given by the clockwise distribution of wooden debris, collapsed piers, and other small structures near the northern tip of the pond.

During times when winds exceed about 10 meters per second, about 15 days of the year, the part of the northward-moving current along the eastern shore of the main part of the pond penetrates the protected northern basin of the pond. It forms a long narrow tongue of foam-banded water along the entire eastern shore, and its pondward contact with calmer water is marked by diminished foam. On 11 August 1964 when the tongue of foam-bonded water was well developed, fluorescent dye patches were placed in lines extending westward from the eastern shore. At the strait the dye patches revealed the maximum northward flow to be on the western side, just off the point. This flow impinged upon the eastern shore in the first 100 meters north of the strait. Dye patches here showed no movement within about 2 meters of shore, evidently because of frictional retardation. Between 2 and about 15 meters from shore the current was directed northward at speeds up to about 2 meters per second. Farther from shore the water moved southward probably toward a convergence with the northward current at the strait, beyond which the southward-flowing current must have passed beneath the northward-flowing one.

In summary, the measurements reveal a counterclockwise current in the main part of the pond and a clockwise one in the northern basin during usual weather conditions. The two sets of currents then form adjacent eddies moving as though geared together. During times of storm winds, however, the current along the eastern side of the main part of the pond penetrates into the northern basin, imposing a counterclockwise current upon the entire pond. The excess water that is driven into the northern basin must leave it by subsurface flow through the strait.

Winds in excess of Beaufort 3 (4 meters per second) develop long parallel slicks on the surface of the pond. The slicks are zones of convergence of surface water between cells caused to rotate by drag of the wind (Woodcock, 1944). In the ocean, oil (probably from phytoplankton) collects along the convergences, smoothing the water surface and changing the light reflectivity and wave pattern. The slicks of the pond are similar in appearance to those of the ocean and they are arranged parallel to the wind, as nearly as can be judged. They are made clearly evident by lines of foam. A second kind of slick was noted during and immediately after heavy rain showers in the absence of wind. This kind is broad and meandering, often having the appearance of puddles. It is presumed that it consists of a thin layer (less than 1 mm) of water from the rain unmixed with that of the pond, and locally changing the properties of the pond surface just as would a thin layer of oil (Ewing, 1950).

WATER LEVEL

The level of the pond fluctuates mostly in response to changes in degree of plugging of its outlet to Vineyard Sound. Wave-induced longshore currents caused by the storms of fall and winter deposit gravel and sand in the outlet. When the pond level is low and the discharge of water from it is small, the gravel and sand makes an effective plug. Occasionally, plugging is also produced by masses of seaweed torn from the shallow sound by storm waves, and during spring by masses of loose pond ice. Plugging from any cause results in a slow rise of pond level until the pond overflows the plug and the effluent is able to erode it away. At times the Falmouth Department of Public Works removes the plug in order to lower the pond level and avoid flooding the cellars of a few houses that were built close to the pond shores. The general effect of plugging and opening of the outlet is the production of alternating periods of slow rise of the pond level followed by periods of more rapid fall of the level (Figs. 18 to 21).

Once when the outlet was dredged (10 January 1964, when the bordering jetties were also lengthened), the shore of the pond was lined with a crust of ice. This crust provided a base-level marker for measuring the southward slope of the pond surface developed by the discharge of water through the outlet. In the first 1000 meters distance from the outlet to the strait at the north, the difference in level was about 6 cm (Fig. 36). The average slope of 6×10^{-5} is considerably greater than would be expected for the discharge of only 0.12 cubic meter per second estimated at the outlet, but perhaps it is a result of bottom friction in the shallow pond.

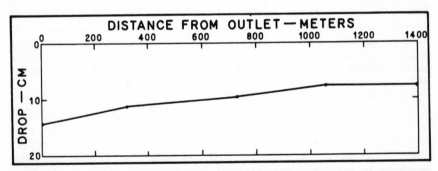

Fig. 36. Drop of water level in Oyster Pond at various distances from its outlet 32 hours after the outlet had been dredged open at 1500 on 10 January 1964. The level was measured from a thin ice crust left attached to pilings or shore rocks along the western side of the pond. The profile extends between the opening to the sound and the north end of the pond.

In addition to its relationship to plugging and opening of the outlet, the level of the pond responds to rains, as shown by an automatic water-level recorder installed on the Emery pier. Excerpts (Fig. 37) from the recordings show that the pond acts essentially as a rain gauge, its level rising approximately the same as the amount of precipitation. When a rain is short and sharp, so is the rise in water level (22 August 1964 of Fig. 37); when the rain lasts throughout a day or more, the pond level also gradually rises (26–28 December 1964). The absence of appreciable stream flow into the pond restricts the after effects of rainfall to the slow influx of ground water. Snowfall atop ice on the pond has the same effect on water level as does rainfall directly on open water.

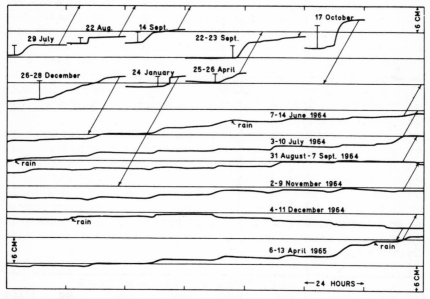

Fig. 37. Sections of water-level recordings measured at the Emery pier near the head of Oyster Pond mostly during 1964. The recordings at the top illustrate the similarity in the rise of pond level to the amount of precipitation measured with a rain-gauge installed next to the water-level recorder. The small T-shaped lines show the amount of precipitation. Longer sections lower on the figure depict the response of the pond to the entrance of sea water during spring tides (essentially an enlargement of the water-level plot of Figs. 18 to 21).

The most frequent and regular change of water level in Oyster Pond is produced by the tides. The water-level recordings show that during times of spring tides, each high tide raises the water level an average of about 1 cm. During the 5 or 6 days of spring tides, the pond level is raised in steps commonly totaling 5 or 6 cm (Figs. 18, 19, 20, 21, and 37). During the intervening neap tides the pond level generally drops in response to the continuously ebbing current. Obviously, the effect of the spring tides is produced only during times when the outlet of the pond is not plugged.

In an effort to learn more about the nature of the exchange of water between Oyster Pond and Vineyard Sound, a 24-hour study was carried out during a time of spring tides. Water levels were measured hourly at several points (seaward end of the jetty at the entrance of the pond system, the railroad conduit, 15 meters landward of the railroad conduit, the highway conduit, and the Emery pier near the head of the pond); currents were measured at the railroad conduit, and temperature and samples for chlorinity measurement were taken 15 meters landward of the railroad conduit. The results (Fig. 38) show that when the tide in Vineyard Sound rose higher than 50 cm above mean low water, the outflow from the pond under the railroad was reversed and a flood current set inward. The reversal in flow direction required 25 minutes to reach the highway conduit; in other words, for a period of 25 minutes water flowed into the two small marsh ponds between Oyster

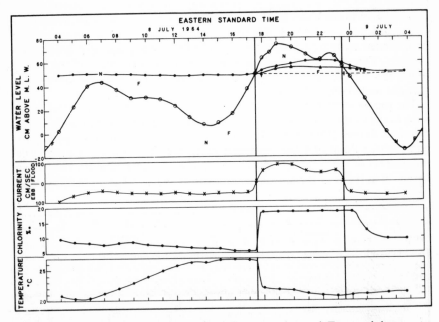

Fig. 38. Results of a 24-hour study of tidal influence on the pond. Top panel shows water level at the seaward end of the jetty (large open circles) adjusted to the best-fit position with respect to predicted tide levels at Nobska Point (N) and Falmouth Heights (F). Water level 15 meters landward of the railroad conduit (small solid dots) rises only when sea level is higher than 50 cm above mean low water. A still smaller amplitude is exhibited by the water-level measurements at the highway conduit (solid triangles) about 260 meters landward of the railroad conduit. Only a 4-mm rise occurred at the head of Oyster Pond (dashed line) and it began about 6 hours after the change of tidal flow near the entrance of the pond. The second panel shows the tidal current through the conduit under the railroad (crosses). The third and fourth panels indicate the chlorinity and temperature at a point 15 meters landward of the railroad conduit. The heavy vertical lines show the times of slack water at the railroad conduit.

Pond and the railroad conduit from both Oyster Pond and Vineyard Sound. About 6 hours elapsed before the turn of tide was detectable at the north end of Oyster Pond. These delays are a measure of the time that is required for the entering water to reverse the seaward slope of the pond system developed during the time of ebbing current, as illustrated by Fig. 36. On the assumption that the water level at a given point in the pond at the time of reversal of flow is approximately equal to that at any other point at the time of its reversal, a common base level of reference can be established. With this method, the water-level measurements at each of the stations were superimposed on the top panel of Fig. 38.

The change from ebb to flood current was marked by an immediate increase in chlorinity and a drop in temperature at the observation point located 15 meters landward from the railroad conduit. The next change, from flood to ebb, was not immediately detectable on the basis of chlorinity and temperature owing to the large quantity of sea water that had accumulated during flood current in the lower reaches of the pond system. In contrast, little of the discharged pond water was able to re-enter the pond system, because it had been carried away by a longshore current of about 5 meters per minute near the jetty. This discharged water is readily noted by swimmers off the nearby beach as a surface layer that is warmer (during the daytime) and more turbid than the underlying sea water.

The top panel of Fig. 38 contains several notations of "F" and "N"; these refer to the times and heights of high and low tide predicted by the Coast and Geodetic Survey (1964) for Falmouth Heights (3.8 km east of the pond jetty) and Nobska Point (2.4 km southwest of it). Owing to the complicated tidal movements of the region (Redfield, 1953), the tides at Falmouth Heights are based upon those of Boston, whereas those of Nobska Point are based upon

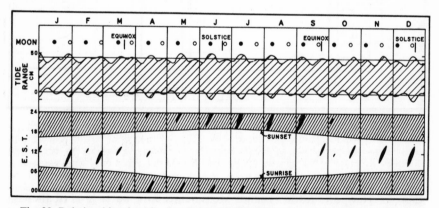

Fig. 39. Relationship of sea level at Falmouth Heights to phases of the moon. When the tide is higher than about 50 cm above mean low water, a flooding current sets into the entrance of Oyster Pond beneath the railroad conduit. These times of flooding current are indicated by the black areas of the bottom panel. The diagram is based upon tidal data for 1964, but diagrams for any other year would be nearly identical.

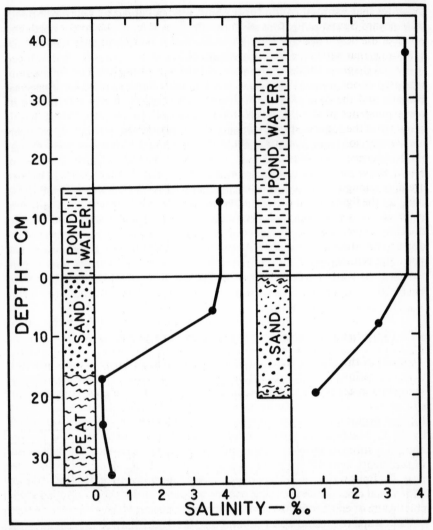

Fig. 40. Salinity of pond and interstitial water of sediments measured by F. T. Manheim, D. A. Ross, and J. D. Milliman on 21 May 1967. Some contamination of the deepest samples by pond water may have occurred during withdrawal of the cores from the bottom. Sites are 5 meters east (left-hand drawing) and 1 meter west of the Emery pier.

those of Newport, Rhode Island. Measurements of water level at the jetty revealed double peaks for each high tide, one corresponding more or less to the prediction for Falmouth Heights and the other for Nobska Point. The base level for the water-level measurements was adjusted to a best-fit position with respect to the predicted points. Though by no means precise, the adjustment indicates that the level of the pond was about 50 cm above mean low water of Vineyard Sound at the time of the study. This level is indicated by the zero point of the height scale in Figs. 18 to 21, and it is the reference level for the soundings that were used for the contours of Fig. 6.

A tidal diagram for the entire year of 1964 was constructed on the basis of tide predictions given by the Coast and Geodetic Survey (1964) for Falmouth Heights and the data of Fig. 38. The results (Fig. 39) reveal a typical close correspondence of the tide range to the dates of full and new moon. It also shows that the highest spring tides are those nearest the dates of the summer and winter solstices. The data reveal that sea water enters the pond due to tidal influence only when the tide in Vineyard Sound is higher than about 50 cm above mean low water. It is evident from Fig. 39 that most spring tides are high enough to cause a flooding current to enter Oyster Pond. In the lower panel of the figure, the dates and hours of these flooding currents are indicated in black. It is assumed that the conduit beneath the railroad is open. The flooding currents occur about noon during the winter and about midnight during the summer. Altogether they are restricted to only about 2% of the year, the remaining 98% of the year having an ebbing current that results from excess water from groundwater leakage and direct precipitation onto the pond.

INTERSTITIAL WATER OF THE SEDIMENTS

Analyses of the ground water adjacent to the shore of Oyster Pond showed it to have a salinity of only 0.1 part per thousand (Table 4). Interstitial waters of sediments in cores of the pond sediment in the nearshore zone (Fig. 40) consist of this same low-salinity ground water extending beneath the pond. Further explorations of the distribution of fresh interstitial waters were made by F. T. Manheim in testing a Schlumberger salinometer adapted for use aboard a submarine. This exploration revealed the presence of fresh water in sediments beneath the pond to a distance of about 15 meters from shore near the Emery pier. A tongue of especially low electrical resistivity, coupled with visual evidence of escaping interstitial water at the shore, may mark the chief route of effluent from a septic tank on the nearby land.

The escape of ground water beyond the shore zone may be prevented by the blanket of fine-grained sediment that lies below about 0.5 meter depth and beyond about 10 meters of the shore. The median grain size at Stations 3 and 18 (Fig. 9) are 4.0 and 8.5 μ, respectively. In accordance with these grain sizes, the water contents are high, 91.4 and 81.5% by wet weight, respectively, in the top 5 cm of bottom sediment. Temperatures of the sediment about 10 cm below the bottom of the pond were found to be as much as 4°C colder during the summer and 4°C warmer during the winter than the immediately overlying bottom water (Fig. 41). This difference may be attributed to poor thermal conduction of the sediment or to bias of sediment temperature by slowly escaping ground water.

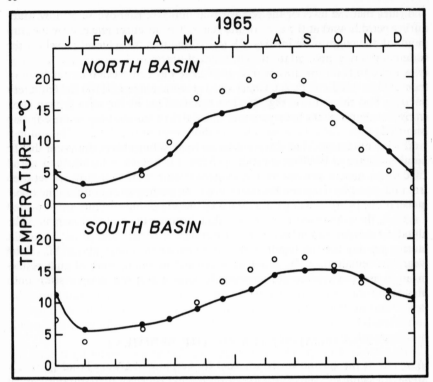

Fig. 41. Annual cycle of temperature about 10 cm below the surface of the bottom sediment (dots and curved line) as compared with the temperature of pond water within 0.5 meter of the bottom (open circles).

WATER BUDGET

The volume of water that is discharged from Oyster Pond to Vineyard Sound can be computed in several ways. One way makes use of the data of Fig. 38 for the 24-hour period of 8–9 July 1964, and the measurements of the cross-sectional area of the conduit that is filled with water. The volume of water leaving the pond was found in this way to be 3370 cubic meters during ebb tide and 1190 cubic meters entered during flood tide. Thus, the net outflow during that period was 2180 cubic meters.

A simpler computation can be made for neap-tide periods when the only flow is seaward from the pond. Sixteen measurements of the seaward flow through the outlet were made between October 1965 and October 1966 at times when the latest precipitation had been at least 2 days earlier. Plotted by month, the data showed discharges that ranged from 7500 cubic meters per day during winter to 200 cubic meters per day during late summer. The annual average discharge was 4400 cubic meters per day.

A third method of computation is based upon the rate of rise of pond level during periods when the outlet is plugged: when no water enters or leaves the pond via the conduit under the railroad. The rise of pond level must be corrected for direct precipitation. Twelve such periods 5 to 53 days long between November 1963 and March 1967 have rates of accumulation ranging from 240 to 4000 cubic meters per day, or an average of 1160 cubic meters per day. This rate is lower than the average obtained by the second method of computation probably because some leakage through the plug in the conduit occurred.

The net discharge from the pond based upon all measurements is probably between 1200 and 4000 cubic meters per day. Let us assume that the average of 2600 cubic meters per day is a reasonable figure. Additional water escapes from the pond by evaporation into the air. According to contours (Knox and Nordenson, 1955) showing the average annual evaporation from lakes of New England, the evaporation loss from a lake at the position of Oyster Pond is about 64 cm per year. This rate corresponds with an average of 400 cubic meters per day for the whole pond. Streams are insignificant and effects of direct precipitation on the pond were avoided by the manner of making the measurements of discharge; therefore, the total of 2600 plus 400, or 3000 cubic meters per day, must represent the discharge by the ground water into the pond. During the 4 years of measurements the total rainfall and snowfall corresponds to a daily average of 500 cubic meters per day for the whole pond, only one sixth of the quantity provided by ground water.

The bottom of the pond is so fine grained that ground water must enter the pond chiefly through shoreline springs. Some is in the form of septic tank and other domestic effluent. Forty-two houses lie within 100 meters of the shore (Fig. 6), but only about half of them are occupied more than the summer months. If we take 175 as the average number of people living in these houses each day of the year and the per capita use of water at 150 gallons per day, the daily domestic use of water is probably less than 100 cubic meters per day, far to small a quantity to account for the net discharge of Oyster Pond. The remaining 2900 cubic meters per day must be from natural ground water at an average rate of about 0.75 cubic meter per meter of inland shoreline per day.

The quantity of ground water discharged by Oyster Pond could be supplied if 83 % of the average annual precipitation of about 115 cm that falls upon the 1.10 square kilometers of drainage area made its way to the ocean as ground water exiting through the pond shorelines. Although this ratio of ground water to total precipitation is high for most land areas, it may be reasonable for the vicinity of Oyster Pond because of the sandy and highly porous nature of the soil.

If Oyster Pond were not present, the total discharge to the ocean of 2900 cubic meters per day of ground water would correspond to about 4 cubic meters per meter of coast per day along the 750-meter frontage of the pond. The remaining 17 % of the precipitation on the drainage area of the pond, presumably lost by evaporation and transpiration, is less than the annual variation in precipitation. Thus decreases in precipitation probably lead to decreases in ground-water discharge that in turn could easily have caused the increase in chlorinity of the pond water during 1965 that is shown by Fig. 26. Presumably, each year of markedly lower than normal precipitation provides a smaller than normal amount of fresh water to flush out the sea water that enters the pond at high tides through its conduit connection with Vineyard Sound.

7 Life

ANIMALS

Oyster Pond contains large numbers of the fresh- and brackish-water *Perca flavescens* (Mitchell)—yellow perch, and *Roccus americanus* (Gmelin)—white perch (really a bass, however). So many are present that the fishes of both species appear to be stunted owing to insufficient food. Of 116 specimens caught by baited hook, the largest was 27 cm and the median length was 17 cm with no appreciable difference in size of the two species. Also caught by baited hook are occasional *Lepomus* sp.—sunfish. The small (5 cm) *Fundulus diaphanus* and others can be caught only with seines. Some fishes enter the pond to spawn. These include *Anguilla rostrata* (Le Sueur)—an eel that lives in the Sargasso Sea during the winter. Several kinds of herring spawn in the pond; chief among them is *Alosa pseudoharingus* (Wilson)—alewife, and *Alosa aestivalis* (Mitchell)—blueback. Some of the herring are caught in nets for roe and pet food as they enter the pond through the conduits at high tides, but most of them reach spawning areas near the head of the pond. The adults spawn in April and May and then depart for the open sea; their progeny leave during late summer.

Reptiles are represented in the pond by numerous turtles; most are about 20 cm long, but one specimen of about 40 cm was seen. Amphibians—frogs of several species—also are present. Mammals that are dependent upon the pond include muskrats and possibly a few otter.

Benthic animals live only in the oxygenated waters less than about 2 meters deep around the shores. The following small forms were identified by G. E. Walsh: *Gammarus fasciatus*—an amphipod, *Scolecolepides viridus*—a polychaete worm, *Hypaniola grayi*—a polychaete worm, an unidentified oligochaete worm, and an unidentified turbellarian flatworm, *Cordylophora lacustris*—a hydroid, and *Hydrobia*—a gastropod.

Among the zooplankton, copepods and tintinnids were noted at the southwestern end of the pond into which the tintinnids at least had probably been carried by currents from the ocean. No foraminiferans were found.

Numerous water birds visit the pond. Most abundant are mallard ducks, several hundred of which are present during the spring and fall migrations; a few remain more or less permanently. As many as 30 Canadian geese stay at the pond for a few days during their migrations. Seagulls, loons and a few fish hawks, herons, and insectivorous birds are commonly present. Several swans nest in the marsh ponds and feed in these ponds and in Oyster Pond.

Among the insects and their larvae are *Hydrochus*—water beetle, water mites, *Lestes*—dragon fly, and Chironomids—midges.

PLANTS

Beginning in April and continuing until November, areas shallower than about 1 meter are partly covered by *Ceratophyllum demersum*—coontail,

63

Potamogeton crispus—pondweed, and *P. foliosus*—leafy pondweed. Also present are *Zannichellia palustris* (?) and *Xyris congdoni* (?). These sessile plants probably comprise a large part of the food supply which makes the pond attractive to birds. During the summer period of greatest growth, masses of the plants break away from the bottom and drift about the pond. Their remains are found on the bottom, to which they contribute organic matter, although probably less than is provided by phytoplankton.

Phytoplankton are abundant in Oyster Pond, giving rise to the greenish color of its water. Perhaps most abundant is the blue-green alga *Microcystis* (or *Anacystis*) *marina*, which also heavily festoons the sessile plants during June and July. Other blue-green algae in the pond are *Anabena*, *Oscillatoria*, and *Merismopedia* (Walsh, 1966). Diatoms, particularly *Chaetoceras*, are present but not abundant. Remains of these plants are deposited on the bottom after staying in suspension for probably several weeks. Five water samples collected on 25 December 1964 at various depths over the southern basin contained 6.5 to 8.9 mg per liter of suspended sediment retained on a 0.45-μ filter. As analyzed by F. T. Manheim, 70 to 83% of the sediment was lost on ashing at 600°C and presumably is organic matter. Examination of the filter under a microscope indicated that the samples from above the halo-cline contained chiefly phytoplankton debris, mostly blue-green algae with only a few diatoms and some pollen and spores. Samples from below the halocline in the oxygen-free water contained only more resistant organic debris such as chitinous skeletal fragments.

BACTERIA

Many kinds of bacteria live in the pond water and sediment as their natural environment. The presence of hydrogen sulfide and methane in the pond indicates the activity of bacteria specifically related to the cycles of these gases. One other form, the photosynthetic bacterium *Chlorobium*, was so abundant near the top of the hydrogen sulfide-rich bottom water of the northern basin during summer that it probably reduced the penetration of sunlight and it materially increased the measured concentration of chlorophyll *a* in the water (Walsh, 1966).

A routine test of the pond water during the spring of 1965 revealed the presence of *Escherichia coli*. Accordingly, two surveys were made in company with R. W. Scannell of the Falmouth Health Department. During the first survey, of 21 July 1965, 12 well-distributed samples of surface water were collected, 6 of which when cultured proved to contain *E. coli* too numerous to count. In a confirming survey of 11 August, 19 water samples included 9 hav-ing *E. coli* too numerous to count. Most other samples of both surveys con-tained measurable numbers of the bacteria. Such concentrations indicated pollution by human excrement, and subsequently an open sewage drain was discovered near the strait between the main basins of the pond. A new survey on 6 July 1966 consisted of 11 samples, of which only one contained con-centrations too numerous to count, although only one sample was completely free of *E. coli*. Finally, a survey on 7 June 1967 indicated 14 samples free of *E. coli* and 4 with only minute traces, such that the water was approved for all domestic purposes by the Barnstable County Health Department. The results of the four surveys clearly show that the circulation of the pond is rapid enough to sweep effluent from a single source throughout the entire pond during the life-span of the bacteria.

PRODUCTIVITY

A knowledge of organic productivity provides information that is necessary for the preparation of an annual budget of organic matter and for integrating the effects of geological, physical, chemical, and biological processes. General interest in the productivity of lakes and oceans has led to the development of many methods of measurement, and several of these methods were applied to Oyster Pond.

Diurnal Cycle of Dissolved Oxygen. One of the most widely used methods of determining organic productivity is to measure the changing concentration of dissolved oxygen at several depths in the water during a 24-hour period. This method also illustrates the influence of plants and animals on the oxygen and carbon dioxide contents of the water. As shown by Fig. 32, photosynthesis during the daytime removes carbon dioxide from the water (raises the pH) and releases oxygen. Respiration of both plants and animals has the opposite effect, and it can be measured at night when photosynthesis cannot occur. The increase of oxygen content in the water during the daytime represents the excess of photosynthesis over respiration. Total volume of oxygen production over oxygen consumption during a 24-hour period is a measure of the net amount of carbon that is removed from carbon dioxide and fixed in plant tissue.

Oxygen dissolved in the water was measured by Winkler titration at 3-hour intervals at the middle of the northern basin and near the shore at the Emery pier in cooperation with G. E. Walsh. As shown by Fig. 32, the measurements at 4 meters in the basin revealed no oxygen present; accordingly, the total volume of oxygen in a 1-square meter column was computed as follows: 0 to 1 meter—uniform at the surface concentration, 1 to 2 meters—simple decline from the surface value to that at 2 meters, and 2 to 3 meters—simple decline from value at 2 meters to zero at 3 meters. At the shore station the oxygen content was assumed to be uniform between the surface and the bottom, which was at a depth of 20 cm. Differences between the volumes of oxygen in a 1 square meter column at 3-hour intervals (Table 5) were due to production by photosynthesis or consumption by respiration during the 3 hours plus some effects of diffusion. Corrections for diffusion across the water surface were made according to the equation (Odum, 1956):

$$O_2 \text{ diffusion} = 0.03 \text{ gm/m}^2/\text{hr}/0.2 \text{ atm}$$

Consumption at night was averaged at 1.20 liters per square meter per 3 hours for the basin, and 0.150 liter per square meter per 3 hours for the shore. These rates of respiratory consumption served to correct net production of oxygen to gross production per 3 hours.

TABLE 5
Productivity Based Upon Changes of Dissolved Oxygen in the Water—31 July and 1 August 1964

Time	O_2 ml/liter 0 m	O_2 ml/liter 2 m	Total O_2 liter/m²	O_2 net production liter/m²/3 hr	O_2 gross production liter/m²/3 hr	Carbon fixed gm/m²/3 hr
North Basin						
06	6.24	4.02	13.38			
				+0.41	1.61	0.72
09	6.44	4.13	13.79			
				+0.24	1.44	0.64
12	6.48	4.31	14.03			
				+1.95	3.15	1.41
15	7.14	5.26	15.97			
				+0.27	1.47	0.66
18	7.55	4.90	16.22			
				−0.12	1.08	0.48
21	7.35	5.06	16.08			
				−1.42	0	0
24	6.38	5.08	14.65			
				−1.15	0	0
03	6.25	4.12	13.50			
				+0.35	1.55	0.69
06	6.19	4.57	13.85			
Total for 24-hour period						4.60
Shore						
06	4.33		0.866			
				+0.562	0.712	0.318
09	7.16		1.432			
				+0.104	0.254	0.113
12	7.60		1.520			
				+0.051	0.201	0.090
15	7.75		1.550			
				+0.072	0.222	0.095
18	8.01		1.602			
				−0.214	0	0
21	6.87		1.374			
				−0.183	0	0
24	5.94		1.188			
				−0.011	0	0
03	5.90		1.180			
				−0.109	0.041	0.018
06	5.39		1.078			
Total for 24-hour period						0.634

The weight of carbon that was fixed each 3 hours (last column of Table 5) can readily be computed on the assumption that 1.00 mole of carbon dioxide is assimilated for every 1.20 moles of oxygen that are liberated (Ryther

1956; Strickland, 1960). The total carbon that was fixed during the 24-hour period, thus, was 4.60 gm per square meter for the basin and 0.63 gm square meter for the shore station.

Multiplication by 8 of the rates of oxygen consumption by respiration per 3 hours and conversion of the product to carbon indicates that the diurnal loss of carbon as carbon dioxide was 4.28 gm for the basin and 0.535 gm for the shore. The difference between gross production and respiration is the net production, 0.32 gm of carbon per day for the basin and 0.099 gm for the shores. This net rate must be much lower, approaching zero, during the winter when the pond is covered by ice.

Changes of Dissolved Oxygen in Light and Dark Bottles. The diurnal cycle of dissolved oxygen can be simulated by the use of light and dark bottles as substitutes for unconfined water. This method avoids complications due to diffusion of oxygen and it permits the making of an estimate of 24-hour productivity using only daytime measurements, but new complications are introduced by the confinement of the water and its plankton. A pair of the light and dark bottles is filled with water and its plankton, and the bottles are suspended at the depth from which the water was collected. After a period the water in each bottle is analyzed for its oxygen concentration. If the bottles are used only during the daytime, as is usual, the oxygen concentration in the dark bottle will have decreased owing to respiration, and that of the light bottle will have increased if photosynthesis was dominant over respiration. The gross production of oxygen due to photosynthesis is the difference in the concentrations of oxygen in the two bottles. Computation of the weight of carbon that was assimilated per unit area per 24 hours is the same as by the previous method.

During the daylight part of the same 24-hour period that organic production was measured by other methods in cooperation with G. E. Walsh, light and dark bottles were analyzed for their oxygen concentrations at 3-hour intervals. The results (Table 6) yielded a value for gross primary productivity over the basin of 4.00 gm of carbon per square meter per day, 87% of that obtained by the previous method. The value for the shore station was 0.19 gm of carbon per square meter per day, only 30% of that by the previous method. The difference in the results by the two methods is attributed partly to the exclusion of sessile algae from the light and dark bottles especially at the shore. In addition, and probably more important, two of the light bottles at each station exhibited a decrease of oxygen content below their initial content (compare Tables 5 and 6). Thus, the gross productions of Table 6 represent minimum values.

Respiration can be estimated from the decrease of oxygen content in the dark bottles below the initial content in the water with which the bottles were filled (Tables 5 and 6). The results of computation of respiration showed a carbon loss of 6.29 gm per square meter per day for the basin and 0.28 gm for the shore. Both values exceed the rate at which carbon is assimilated by photosynthesis according to Table 6, again indicating that the gross productivity must be greater than indicated by Table 6.

TABLE 6
Productivity Based Upon Changes of Dissolved Oxygen in Light and Dark Bottles—
31 July and 1 August 1964

Time	O_2 ml/liter			O_2 Gross production liter/m²/3 hr	Carbon fixed gm/m²/3 hr
	Light	Dark	Difference		
North Basin					
06					
	6.53	6.14	0.39	0.78	0.35
09					
	6.23	6.07	0.16	0.32	0.14
12					
	6.60	5.03	1.57	3.14	1.40
15					
	7.27	5.19	2.08	4.16	1.86
18					
	7.30	7.02	0.28	0.56	0.25
21					
Total for 24-hour period					4.00
Shore					
06					
	4.68	4.15	0.53	0.106	0.047
09					
	6.91	6.61	0.30	0.060	0.027
12					
	8.04	7.46	0.58	0.116	0.152
15					
	8.28	7.64	0.64	0.128	0.057
18					
	7.09	7.02	0.07	0.014	0.006
21					
Total for 24-hour period					0.189

Assimilation of Radiocarbon. A common method of determining net productivity of phytoplankton is to add a measured quantity of C^{14}-labeled bicarbonate to water samples and suspend them at the original depth of collection for several hours. Afterward, the samples are filtered and the amount of C^{14} that was added to the cells by photosynthesis is measured with a Geiger counter (Strickland and Parsons, 1960, pp. 153–163).

Using this method, C. S. Yentsch measured the C^{14} assimilation above the southern basin during a winter day when the pond was covered with 23 cm of ice topped with 2.5 cm of snow. Computation was as follows:

$$\mu\text{g C/liter/hr} = \frac{(L-D)_{\text{CPM}} \times 0.0054}{T}$$

where $(L-D)_{\text{CPM}}$ is the difference in the counts per minute in the filtered plankton from the light and from the dark bottles, 0.0054 is a factor that includes the C^{14} dosage, and T is the duration of the photosynthesis after dosage—4.67 hours in this experiment. The results (Table 7) yielded a net

TABLE 7

Productivity Based Upon Uptake of C^{14} in Light and Dark Bottles in Southern Basin of Oyster Pond—5 February 1965

Depth m	Counts per Minute in light-dark bottles	μg C/liter/hr	μg C/liter/day[1]	mg C/m²/day
0[2]	n.d.	0.900	7.200	
				5.64
1	437	0.509	4.072	
				2.60
2	122	0.142	1.136	
				1.02
3	97	0.113	0.904	
				0.62
4	37	0.042	0.337	
				0.17
5[2]	n.d.			—
Total net productivity for 24-hour period				10.05

[1] Effective photosynthesis was limited to about 8 hours of day.
[2] By extrapolation of other values.

productivity of 0.010 gm of carbon per square meter per day. This is a very low productivity, as might be expected from the presence of an ice and snow cover and the low temperature of the water.

Production of Dissolved Carbohydrate. Dissolved carbohydrate is a metabolic product of living organisms as well as a breakdown product of dead organic matter. Eventually it serves as an energy source for other plants or bacteria and its content of carbon is returned to the water as carbon dioxide. As shown by Fig. 32, the dissolved carbohydrate is most abundant at the time of day when the primary productivity is greatest. Obviously, the carbon in dissolved carbohydrate must be only a fraction of the total amount of carbon that is fixed by photosynthesis, but that fraction may serve as a general indicator of the total primary productivity.

During the 24-hour experiment of 31 July and 1 August 1964, Walsh (1965b) measured the concentrations of dissolved carbohydrate in the water at 0 and 2 meters depth at the northern basin and at the shore station. He also measured the concentrations in light and dark bottles placed near the surface at both locations. The results (Fig. 32) can be totaled for the 24-hour period using the same methods as were used for dissolved oxygen. Values for production of dissolved carbohydrate over the basin and at the shore were 6.33 and 0.70 gm per square meter per day on the basis of measurements in the water, and they were 8.28 and 0.90 gm per square meter per day on the basis of light and dark bottle measurements. Taking 40% as a reasonable content of carbon in dissolved carbohydrate, the total amounts of carbon that were released in the form of carbohydrate over the basin and at the shore were 2.53 and 0.28 gm per square meter per day on the basis of the water measurements, and they were 3.30 and 0.36 gm per square meter per day on the basis of light and dark bottle measurements. These values suggest that the carbon released in dissolved carbohydrate may be about half of the total carbon that was assimilated by photosynthesis during the same 24-hour period (Tables 5 and 6).

During part of a year-long study based upon weekly samples, Walsh (1966) found that afternoon concentrations of dissolved carbohydrate were greater than morning concentrations. This difference must be due to the daytime release of dissolved carbohydrate from cells. On the basis of the average daily release, Walsh determined that about 119 mg of dissolved carbohydrate per liter per year were produced. This quantity contains about 47.7 mg of carbon per liter per year. For the entire 4-meter depth at the site, the total annual release of carbon in the form of dissolved carbohydrate must be about 190 gm. If half of the total assimilated carbon is released in dissolved carbohydrate, the total carbon fixed by photosynthesis must be about 380 gm per square meter per year over the northern basin.

Chlorophyll a. Studies of productivity in the field and laboratory by Ryther and Yentsch (1957) showed that the gross productivity of marine and non-marine phytoplankton can be determined from measurements of chlorophyll *a*. According to their work

$$P = \frac{R}{k} \times C \times 3.7$$

where *P* is the productivity in grams of carbon per square meter per day, *R* is the relative photosynthesis derived from their experimental curve (their Fig. 1) for which langleys of radiation are required, *k* is the light extinction coefficient of the water, *C* is chlorophyll *a* in grams per cubic meter, and 3.7 is an experimental constant that shows the ratio of carbon assimilated to the concentration of chlorophyll *a*. *R* can be determined from solar radiation that was measured at Woods Hole during 1962 by C. S. Yentsch; $k = 1.7/D$, where *D* is the monthly average depth of Secchi disk readings at Oyster Pond (the *k* values computed from the Secchi disk measurements are at the same general level as *k* from light-meter measurements of Fig. 34); and *C* is the surface concentration of chlorophyll *a* in micrograms per liter over the northern basin by Walsh (1966). All of these parameters were averaged by months and are listed in Table 8.

Using the formula above, the average daily productivity was computed, combined into monthly productivity, and totalled as annual gross productivity. The final value was found to be 140 gm of carbon per square meter per year. Probably this value is low because the chlorophyll *a* was extracted by Walsh from water samples in which the cells were not broken by grinding (Strickland and Parsons, 1960, pp. 107–112). Analyses by Yentsch for most of the same period and made upon finely ground cells yielded concentrations of chlorophyll *a* approximately 2.5 times those of Walsh (Fig. 29). Thus an annual gross productivity over the northern basin of about 350 gm per square meter is taken as the most reasonable value obtainable from existing measurements of chlorophyll *a* in Oyster Pond.

TABLE 8
Productivity Based upon Measurements of Chlorophyll *a* at the Water Surface Over
the Northern Basin during 1964

Month	Surface radiation langleys	R	Average Secchi disk depths—m	k	C μg/liter	P gm C/m²/day	Days per month	P gm C/m²/mo
J	175	12.2	142	1.20	2.68	0.101	31	3.1
F	240	15.0	129	1.32	16.90	0.710	29	20.6
M	350	18.4	118	1.44	14.21	0.673	31	20.8
A	435	20.8	109	1.56	6.85	0.338	30	10.1
M	500	22.4	103	1.65	5.89	0.296	31	9.2
J	520	23.0	100	1.70	7.02	0.351	30	10.5
J	505	22.6	98	1.73	9.31	0.450	31	14.0
A	425	20.6	98	1.73	11.97	0.527	31	16.3
S	320	18.0	102	1.66	8.57	0.344	30	10.3
O	230	14.8	108	1.57	9.51	0.332	31	10.3
N	180	12.2	115	1.48	8.75	0.267	30	8.0
D	155	11.5	127	1.34	6.43	0.204	31	6.3
Total for year								139.5

Cropping of Attached Algae. During August 1964 when the shore algae were at their peak of growth, all vegetation in a 1-meter square near the Emery pier was removed, dried, and weighed. The dry weight was 109 gm. About 46% (Ryther, 1956) of this weight is carbon; thus the carbon in the standing crop of sessile algae in the shore zone was approximately 50 gm per square meter. Because the collection was made near the maximum extent of the algae, this figure for the standing crop must nearly equal that for gross annual productivity of the shore zone. It is much lower than the gross annual productivity of phytoplankton in the pond except near the shore where the water is shallow.

BUDGET OF ORGANIC CARBON

The gross annual productivity of Oyster Pond is a very uncertain quantity, as shown in the previous section. The results from all measurements of productivity in the northern basin have been drawn together in Table 9. They show that the gross diurnal productivity is far greater than in the open ocean (Strickland, 1960, pp. 96–99), and that it lies in the same general range as the productivity of shallow Texas bays (Odum and Wilson, 1962). A reasonable figure for the gross annual productivity is 400 gm per square meter. This is much higher than the 55 to 70 gm that is accepted for the mean gross annual productivity for all oceans (Duursma, 1963). Along the shore of Oyster Pond the productivity is lower than above the northern basin, but in most of the southern basin the depth of water is greater than in the northern basin, leading to a higher value for productivity; thus the rate for the whole pond may be near the same as that for the northern basin alone.

TABLE 9
Summary of Productivity Measurements for the Northern Basin of Oyster Pond

| Method | gm C/m²/day | | | gm C/m²/year |
	Gross production	Respiration	Net production	Gross production
Diurnal cycle of dissolved oxygen (July)	4.60	4.28	0.32	
Changes of dissolved oxygen in light and dark bottles (July)	4.00+	6.29		
Assimilation of radiocarbon (February)			0.01	
In dissolved carbohydrate of the open water (July)	2.53			(380)
In light and dark bottles (July)	3.30			
Content of chlorophyll *a*	0.10–0.71			(350)

Some of the carbon that is assimilated by plants and later released by them is flushed out of the pond in particulate or dissolved form. The concentration of these materials in the pond water is probably about 8 mg per liter, and, as shown in the section on the water budget, the discharge of the pond averages about 3100 cubic meters per day (2600 from ground water inflow plus 500 from direct precipitation onto the pond). This concentration of organic carbon and rate of water discharge corresponds with an annual loss of organic carbon from the pond amounting to about 9 million grams (9 tons) per year, or 36 gm per square meter of the pond surface per year.

Additional loss of carbon occurs through burial within the bottom sediments. As discussed in the section on sediments, the radiocarbon ages of sections along a drill hole in the northern basin yield a rate of deposition of total dry sediment amounting to about 38 mg per square centimeter per year. Organic carbon constitutes 16% of the weight of these sediments; therefore, the loss of carbon to the bottom of this basin is 4.5 mg per square centimeter per year, or 45 gm per square meter per year. This is probably about the same as the average rate of loss for the entire pond, because the sediments of the northern basin contain more organic carbon than do those elsewhere in the pond (Fig. 11), but they also are deposited more slowly than in the southern basin (Figs. 15 and 16). A reasonable average rate of loss of carbon to the bottom probably is thus about 40 gm per square meter per year.

The foregoing computations show that of the 400 gm per square meter of annual assimilation of carbon by plant photosynthesis, 36 gm are lost to the ocean in the water that overflows from Oyster Pond, and 40 gm are lost to the bottom sediment. The difference, 324 gm, is the annual loss by respiration or related functions. Nearly all of it occurs probably within a few days after its original assimilation. Probably the carbon that is lost to the ocean in overflow also is soon used and converted to carbon dioxide, so that the only semi-permanent storage of the carbon that is assimilated by plants is that 10% which is buried in the sediments. Fortunately, this carbon contains within it much of the record of the pond.

8 Summary

The history of Oyster Pond can be traced to perhaps 14,000 years ago when the huge mass of glacial ice that extended to Martha's Vineyard from the colder and higher lands to the north began to wane. Isolated tongues of ice remained partly buried under rock wastes released by the melting of the main mass of the glaciers. When finally about 12,500 years ago, the ice was gone from the area, its last position was marked by a long valley having an irregular floor. Two parts that were deeper than the rest contained water from melted ice, snow, and rain. Sands and silts from the bare surface of the glacial moraine washed into the valley and its two ponds. Soon grasses and later spruce and pine forests covered the earth and permitted only silt and clay to reach the ponds along with debris from the plants themselves. The ocean 12,000 years ago still lay far beyond the present Vineyard Sound, but, as the glaciers of the world continued to melt and return their borrowed water to the ocean, the sea level rose until, about 3000 years ago, its waters spilled into the southern pond and 2200 years ago into the northern one. Henceforth, the remains of marine organisms replaced those of fresh-water ones to be mixed on the floor of the pond with the debris of land plants, largely oaks by that time.

About 11,500 years ago bands of hunters who used fluted projectile points appeared on the scene, to be supplanted thousands of years later by Indians who achieved a farming economy about 1000 years ago. The Indians' corn, pumpkins, squash, and beans were immediately adopted by the first permanent European settlers on their arrival about 350 years ago. Rapid clearing of the land by the settlers for farming, sheep herding, and fuel replaced the forests with open fields surrounded with stone fences until farming became uneconomical in the region about 50 years ago.

Oyster Pond served the settlers as a source of oysters and of fish, particularly herring. About 200 years ago the longshire drift of sand and gravel formed a baymouth bar that nearly closed the connection of the pond with the adjacent sound. The inflow of ocean water was so reduced that the salinity of the pond became too low to support the oysters. Thereafter, the pond's chief value to man was for recreation and shore building sites—a use that began in earnest only about 20 years ago.

Nearness of the pond to the several marine institutions at Woods Hole permits it to serve a rather unique function—as a model environment for investigating processes of sedimentation, water mechanics, and biogeochemistry with modern techniques. The interest is enhanced by the presence of a deep area that usually contains a submerged puddle of water having a much greater salinity than the overlying water. Its density isolates the salty puddle from all except the most violent movements of the surface water, and so during most of the year it is stagnant—devoid of dissolved oxygen.

The pond overflows to the ocean about 98 % of the time, because precipitation plus ground-water inflow through shoreline springs greatly exceeds evaporation from the pond surface. As a result, a daily average of about 3100 cubic meters of water overflows from the pond to the ocean. Expressed in other terms, the ground-water inflow to the pond corresponds to about 4 cubic meters per day per linear meter of marine shoreline in front of the pond. This high rate is due to the sandy and highly permeable nature of the glacial till on Cape Cod. During the exceptionally dry year 1965, the inflow of ground water into the pond was so reduced that it was unable to flush out the ocean water that entered at high spring tides during about 2% of the year. The salinity more than doubled during that year, to diminish again to its usual 5% of the value in the open ocean when the rainfall increased during the following year.

Surface water of the pond circulates in response to the wind, and it moves counterclockwise, as does that of most lakes and seas in the northern hemisphere. Only a few days are required for the circuit to be completed. In spite of the speed of this wind-driven circulation, a 5% seaward gradient of salinity in the pond is maintained by the inflow of ground water mainly at the landward end and by the intermittent inflow of ocean water only at the seaward end of the pond.

Ice on the pond reaches a thickness of 25 cm during winter, and it serves as an insulating cover that reduces the heat loss from the water. Consequently, the temperature of the underlying water increases during the winter through conduction from the bottom, oxidation of organic matter, and inflow of ground water. Melting in the spring probably occurs from both above and below the ice sheet. The ice cover also reduces the quantity of sunlight that can penetrate the water, so that photosynthesis is much reduced during the winter months.

Little benthic animal life is present except along the pond shores. In contrast, so many fishes live in the pond that their requirements exceed their food supply at least seasonally, so that they have become somewhat dwarfed. The base of the food pyramid for all animals is the very abundant planktonic algae that impart a light green color to the water and that have an annual primary productivity of about 400 gm of carbon per square meter per year. Most of this organic carbon is oxidized to carbon dioxide through respiration by the plants and animals that live in the pond. Somewhat less than 10% of it is carried to the ocean within the overflowing water from the pond, and a bit more than 10% of it is buried in the bottom sediment each year. Because of the high productivity and the incomplete oxidation of the organic debris, the bottom sediments contain a rich assemblage of amino acids, sugars, and many other organic compounds whose future study may provide much biochemical interest.

At the rate at which bottom sediments have been deposited during the past 2000 years, Oyster Pond can remain a body of water for about 4000 years more if the sea level remains about the same as now and if man's activities do not materially alter the pond. We can hope that for some of these years this and other similar ponds will remain to be enjoyed in scientific studies as well as for esthetic and recreational purposes.

References

Baas Becking, L. G. M., Kaplan, I. R., and Moore, D., 1960. Limits of the natural environment in terms of pH and oxidation-reduction potentials. *J. Geol.*, 68: 243–284.

Bloom, A. L., 1963. Late Pleistocene fluctuations of sea level and post-glacial rebound in coastal Maine. *Amer. J. Sc.*, 261: 862–879.

Board of Trade and Industry (C. H. Washburn, Editor), 1896. *Falmouth-by-the-Sea: The Naples of America.* Privately printed, Falmouth, 214 pp.

Clarke, G. E., and Holton, S. A., 1887. *The Celebration of the Two Hundredth Anniversary of the Incorporation of the Town of Falmouth, Massachusetts.* L. F. Clarke Co., Falmouth, 133 pp.

Coast and Geodetic Survey, 1953. Density of sea water at tide stations, Atlantic Coast and and South America. *Spec. Publ.* No. 279, 62 pp.

Coast and Geodetic Survey, 1955. Surface water temperatures at tide stations, Atlantic Coast North and South America *Spec. Publ.* No. 278: 69 pp.

Coast and Geodetic Survey, 1957. Density of sea water at tide stations, Atlantic Coast North and South America. *Publ.* 31–2: 72 pp.

Coast and Geodetic Survey, 1960. Surface water temperature and salinity, Atlantic Coast North and South America. *Publ.* 31–1: 76 pp.

Coast and Geodetic Survey, 1964. Tide tables, high and low water predictions, 1962: East Coast North and South America including Greenland: U.S. Department of Commerce, 285 pp.

Day, C. G., 1959. Oceanographic observations, 1959. East coast of the United States: *U.S. Fish Wildlife Serv., Spec. Sci. Rep.—Fisheries* No. 359: 114 pp.

Day, C. G., 1963. Oceanographic observations, 1960. East coast of the United States: *U.S. Fish Wildlife Serv., Spec. Sci. Rep.—Fisheries* No. 406; 59 pp.

Deevey, E. S., Jr., 1948. On the date of the last rise of sea level in southern New England, with remarks on the Grassy Island site. *Amer. J. Sci.* 246: 329–352.

Degens, E. T., Emery, K. O., and Reuter, J. H., 1963. Organic materials in recent and ancient sediments, Pt. III: Biochemical compounds in San Diego Trough, California. *N. Jb. Geol. Paläontol*, Mh., No. 5: 231–248.

Degens, E. T., Prashnowsky, A., Emery, K. O., and Pimenta, J., 1961. Organic materials in recent and ancient sediments, Pt. II: Amino acids in marine sediments of Santa Barbara Basin, California: *N. Jb. Geol. Paläontol.*, Mh., No. 8: 413–426.

Deyo, S. L. (Editor), 1890. *History of Barnstable County, Massachusetts.* H. W. Blake & Co., New York, 1010 pp.

Duursma, E. K., 1963. The production of dissolved organic matter in the sea, as related to the primary gross production of organic matter. *Netherlands J. Sea Res.*, 2: 85–94.

Emerson, Amelia F., 1935. *Early History of Naushon Island.* Thomas Todd Co., Boston, 502 pp.

Emerson, B. K., 1917. Geology of Massachusetts and Rhode Island. *U.S. Geol. Survey, Bull.* 597: 289 pp.

Emery, K. O., 1960. *The Sea off Southern California: A Modern Habitat of Petroleum.* Wiley, New York, 366 pp.

Emery, K. O., Wigley, R. L., and Rubin, Meyer, 1965. A submerged peat deposit off the Atlantic coast of the United States. *Limnol. Oceanogr. Suppl.* 10: 97–102.

Ewing, G., 1950. Slicks, surface films and internal waves. *J.Marine Res.*, 9: 161–187.

Ewing, Maurice, Crary, A. P., and Rutherford, H. M., 1937. Geophysical investigations in the emerged and submerged Atlantic Coastal Plain, Part I. *Bull. Geol. Soc. Amer.*, 48: 753–802.

Faught, M. C., 1945. *Falmouth, Massachussetts: Problems of a Resort Community.* Columbia Univ. Press, New York, 130 pp.

Forbes, 1934.

Freeman, Frederick, 1862. *The History of Cape Cod.* Rand & Avery, Boston, 2 vols.

Galtsoff, P. S., 1962. The story of the bureau of commercial fisheries biological laboratory, Woods Hole Massachusetts: *Bur. Comm. Fisheries, Circ.* 145: 121 pp.

Geoffrey, Theodate, 1930. *Suckanesset, Wherein May be Read a History of Falmouth, Massachusetts.* Falmouth Publ. Co., Inc., 168 pp.

Goddard, E. N., and others, 1948. *Rock-Color Chart.* National Research Council, Washington, D. C.

Gookin, W. F., and Barbour, P. L., 1963. *Bartholomew Gosnold, Discoverer and Planter. New England—1602, Virginia—1607.* Archon Books, Hamden, Conn., 271 pp.

Gray, Edwin, 1944. *The Hurricane in Pictures, 1944, Falmouth, Cape Cod.* Falmouth, Mass., 50 pp.

Howe, H. F., 1943. *Prologue to New England; The Forgotten Century of the Explorers.* Farrar & Rinehart, New York, 324 pp.

Jenkins, C. W., 1889. *Three Lectures on the Early History of the Town of Falmouth Covering the Time from Its Settlement to 1812, Delivered in the Year 1843.* L. F. Clarke Co., Falmouth, 111 pp.

Kanwisher, J. W., 1962. Gas exchange of shallow marine sediments: The Environmental Chemistry of Marine Sediments. Proc. of a Symposium Held at the Univ. Rhode Island on 13 Jan. 1962. *Occ. Publ. Narragansett Marine Lab.* No. 1: 13–19.

Kaplan, I. R., Emery, K. O., and Rittenberg, S. C., 1963. The distribution and isotopic abundance of sulphur in recent marine sediments off southern California. *Geochim. Cosmochim. Acta,* 27: 297–331.

Kaye, C. A., 1964. Outline of Pleistocene geology of Martha's Vineyard. *U.S. Geol. Survey, Prof. Paper* 501–C: 134–139.

Kaye, C. A., and Barghoorn, E. S., 1964. Late Quaternary sea-level change and crustal rise in Boston, Massachusetts, with notes on the autocompaction of peat. *Bull. Geol. Soc. Amer.* 75: 63–80.

Kittredge, H. C., 1930. *Cape Cod, Its People and Their History.* Houghton Mifflin, New York, 330 pp.

Knox, C. E., and Nordenson, T. J., 1955. Average annual runoff and preciptiation in the New England–New York area. *U.S. Geol. Survey Hydrol. Invest. Atlas* HA 7.

Koyama, T., 1963. Gaseous metabolism in lake sediments and paddy soils and the production of atmospheric methane and hydrogen: *J. Geophys. Res.* 68: 3971–3973.

Landegren, S., 1954. On the relative abundance of the stable carbon isotopes in marine sediments. *Deep-Sea Res.* 1: 89–120.

Ludlum, D. M., 1963. *Early American Hurricanes, 1492–1870.* Amer. Meterol. Soc., Boston, 198 pp.

Mather, K. F., Goldthwait, R. P., and Thiesmeyer, L. R., 1942. Pleistocene geology of western Cape Cod, Massachusetts: *Bull. Geol. Soc. Amer.,* 53: 1127–1174.

Medcof, J. C., Clarke, A. H., Jr., and Erskine, J. S., 1965. Ancient Canadian east-coast oyster and quahaug shells. *J. Fisheries Board Canada,* 22: 631–634.

Menzel, D. W., and Vaccaro, R. F., 1964. The measurement of dissolved organic and particulate carbon in seawater. *Limnol. Oceanog.,* 9: 138–142.

Merrill, A. S., Emery, K. O., and Rubin, Meyer, 1965. Ancient oyster shells on the Atlantic continental shelf. *Science,* 147: 398–400

Odum, H. T., 1956. Primary production in flowing waters. *Limnol. Oceanog.,* 1: 102–117.

Odum, H. T., and Wilson, R. F., 1962. Further studies on reaeration and metabolism of Texas bays, 1958–1960. *Publ. Inst. Marine Sci.* 8: 23–55.

Ogden, J. G., III, 1963. The Squibnocket cliff peat: Radiocarbon dates and pollen stratigraphy. *Amer. J. Sci.* 261: 344–353.

Oldale, R. N., and Tuttle, C. R., 1964. Seismic investigations on Cape Cod, Massachusetts. *U.S. Geol. Survey, Prof. Paper* 465–D: 118–122.

Redfield, A. C., 1953. Interference phenomena in the tides of the Woods Hole region. *J. Marine Res.* 12: 121–140.

Redfield, A. C., and Miller, A. R., 1957. Water levels accompanying Atlantic coast hurricanes. *Meteorol. Monogr.* 2 (10): 1–23.

Redfield, A. C., and Rubin, M., 1962. The age of salt marsh peat and its relation to recent changes in sea level at Barnstable, Massachusetts. *Proc. Natl. Acad. Sci., U.S.,* 48: 1728–1735.

Ross, D. A., 1967. Heavy-mineral assemblages in the nearshore surface sediments of the Gulf of Maine. *U.S. Geol. Survey Prof. Paper 575-C; C77-C80.*

Rubin, Meyer, and Alexander, Corrinne, 1960. U.S. Geological Survey radiocarbon dates V. *Amer. J. Sci Radiocarbon Suppl.*, 2: 129–185.

Ryther, J. H., 1956. The measurement of primary productivity. *Limnol. Oceanog.*, 1, 72–84.

Ryther, J. H., and Yentsch, C. S., 1957. The estimation of phytoplankton production in the ocean from chlorophyll and light data. *Limnol. Oceanog.*, 11; 281–286.

Sackett, W. M., 1964. The depositional history and isotopic organic carbon composition of marine sediments. *Marine Geol.* 2: 173–185.

Sackett, W. M., Eckelmann, W. R., Bender, M. L., and Bé, A. W. H., 1965. Temperature dependence of carbon isotope composition in marine plankton and sediments. *Science*, 148: 235–237.

Schlee, John, 1966. A modified Woods Hole rapid sediment analyzer: *J. Sedimentary Petrol.* 36: 403–413.

Shaler, N. S., 1897. Geology of the Cape Cod district. *U.S. Geol. Survey, Ann. Rept.*, 18, pt. 2: 497–593.

Silverman, S. R., and Epstein, Samuel, 1958. Carbon isotopic compositions of petroleum and other sedimentary organic materials: *Bull. Amer. Assoc. Petroleum Geologists*, 42: 998–1012.

Strickland, J. D. H., 1960. Measuring the production of marine phytoplankton. *Fisheries Res. Board Canada, Bull.* 122: 172 pp.

Strickland, J. D. H., and Parsons, T. R., 1960. A manual of sea water analysis (with special reference to the more common micronutrients and to particulate organic material). *Fisheries Res. Board Canada, Bull.* 125: 185 pp.

Sverdrup, H. U., Johnson, M. W., and Fleming, R. H., 1942. *The Oceans*. Prentice-Hall, New York, 1087 pp.

Walsh, G. E., 1965a. Studies on dissolved carbohydrate in Cape Cod waters. I. General survey. *Limnol. Oceanog.* 10: 570–576.

Walsh, G. E., 1965b. Studies on dissolved carbohydrate in Cape Cod waters. II. Diurnal fluctuation in Oyster Pond. *Limnol. Oceanog.* 10: 577–582.

Walsh, G. E., 1966. Studies on dissolved carbohydrate in Cape Cod waters. III. Seasonal variation in Oyster Pond and Wequaquet Lake, Massachusetts. *Limnol. Oceanog.*, 11: 249–256.

Walton, Perry, 1925. *Falmouth of Cape Cod, Picturesque, Romantic, Historic* (2nd ed.). Perry Walton, Boston, 47 pp.

Washburn, C. H., 1897. *Residential Falmouth*. Rockwell and Churchill Press, Boston, 96 pp.

Weather Bureau, 1961. Local climatological data, Nantucket Mass., 4 pp.

Woodcock, A. H., 1944. A theory of surface water motion deduced from the wind-induced motion of the Physalia. *J. Marine Res.*, 5: 196–205.

Woodcock, A. H., 1965. Melt patterns in ice over shallow waters. *Limnol. Oceanog. Suppl.* 10: 290–297.

Woodworth, J. B., and Wigglesworth, E., 1934. Geography and geology of the region including Cape Cod, the Elizabeth Islands, Nantucket, Martha's Vineyard, No Man's Land and Block Island. *Mus. Comp. Zool., Mem.* 52: 322 pp.

Yentsch, C. S., and Menzel, D. W., 1963. A method for the determination of phytoplankton chlorophyll and phaeophytin by fluorescence. *Deep-Sea Res.* 10: 221–231.

Zeigler, J. M., Hoffmeister, W. S., Giese, Graham, and Tasha, Herman, 1960. Discovery of Eocene sediments in subsurface of Cape Cod. *Science*, 132, 1397–1398.

Index